MOVING IN

MOVING IN

BUYING, SELLING AND RENTING YOUR HOME

SARA McCONNELL

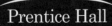

Prentice Hall

an imprint of Pearson Education

London • New York • San Francisco • Toronto • Sydney • Tokyo • Singapore
Hong Kong • Cape Town • Madrid • Paris • Milan • Munich • Amsterdam

PEARSON EDUCATION LIMITED

Head Office:
Edinburgh Gate
Harlow CM20 2JE
Tel: +44 (0)1279 623623
Fax: +44 (0)1279 431059

London Office:
128 Long Acre
London WC2E 9AN
Tel: +44 (0)20 7447 2000
Fax: +44 (0)20 7240 5771
Website: www.business-minds.com

First published in Great Britain in 2002

The right of Sara McConnell to be identified as Author of this Work has been asserted by her in accordance with the Copyright, Designs and Patents Act 1988.

ISBN 0 273 65684 8

British Library Cataloguing in Publication Data
A CIP catalogue record for this book can be obtained from the British Library

This publication is designed to provide accurate and authoritative information in regard to the subject matter covered. It is sold with the understanding that neither the author nor the publisher is engaged in rendering legal, investing, or any other professional service. If legal advice or other expert assistance is required, the service of a competent professional person should be sought.

10 9 8 7 6 5 4 3 2 1

Designed by Claire Brodmann Book Designs, Lichfield, Staffs
Typeset by Northern Phototypesetting Co Ltd, Bolton
Printed and bound in Great Britain by Biddles Ltd, Guildford & King's Lynn

The Publishers' policy is to use paper manufactured from sustainable forests.

ABOUT THE AUTHOR

Sara McConnell is an award-winning freelance property journalist who writes for a range of national newspapers including the London *Evening Standard* and the *Sunday Telegraph*. Her work has also been published in *The Times*, *Daily Mail* and *Daily Telegraph* and she is a regular commentator on property issues on television and radio. She lives in South London with her partner and their young son.

CONTENTS

Introduction xi

....

1 Buying 1

Where do you start? 2

Starting your search 3

Get the area lowdown 3

How to spot an up and coming area 9

How to deal with estate agents 12

Prices are rising – no they're not 20

Viewing properties 21

Making an offer 27

....

2 Selling 30

How to choose an estate agent 32

How much is your home worth? 34

When to put your property on the market 39

Agree terms 40

How much do agents charge? 41

Selling your home on the internet 42

Fresh brewed coffee and home-baked bread? 45

Getting an offer 49

....

3 The buying and selling process 54

How the system works now – England and Wales 56

How the future could look – England and Wales 75

The Scottish system 78

4 **Your finances** 82

Workings of the mortgage market 84

What to look for 85

Checklist 91

CAT marks 94

Strapped for cash or complex case? 95

Repayment methods explained 98

Which investment? 99

Where to shop for your mortgage 103

A dog's dinner? Mortgage regulation 109

What to expect under the code 112

Applying for your loan 112

Protecting your mortgage repayments 115

5 **New homes** 118

Buying a new home 120

How the new build buying system works 122

The selling of a lifestyle – is it you? 128

NHBC – warranty not guarantee 130

Self build – can you face it? 132

6 **Moving house and home improvements** 136

Planning your moving arrangements 138

Your main tasks 140

Removals 141

Contact utilities 144

Home improvements 146

Planning matters 149

Do you need planning permission? 150

7 Renting and letting 154

Renting 156

Landlords versus tenants 159

Tenants 159

Landlords 173

Buy to let 180

8 Off the wall ways to buy, sell and rent 186

House swapping 188

Auctions 191

Buying overseas 196

Glossary 201

Useful websites 208

Index 215

INTRODUCTION

A nightmare system

Selling and/or buying a house
should be simple

Selling and/or buying a house should be simple. You put your existing home on the market (exaggerating its charms just enough to get queues forming at the door and not enough to get sued later on) and find a buyer. At the same time you find a property you want to move to. Solicitors for both sides shuffle papers around and draw up contracts which they then exchange, binding both sides to the deal. Then you all pay over large sums of money and get the keys to the homes of your dreams. Easy? If only. Property writers love to repeat the cliché that moving house is one of life's most stressful events, beaten only by bereavement, divorce and Christmas. But as anyone who has ever done it will tell you, stressful doesn't begin to describe the hell of housebuying, at least in England and Wales (the Scots have a different system, which makes huge amounts of money for surveyors and solicitors in the guise of giving buyers and sellers early certainty that the deal will go through).

Stressful doesn't begin
to describe the hell of
housebuying

Why is the whole process in England and Wales so awful? You'll hear lots of individual horror stories but many of them stem from one or more of the following:

- Most people need to sell their existing home in order to fund their new one, whose owners in turn need to sell theirs to pay for their move … and so on, ad infinitum. This is known as the chain and nothing strikes dread into the hearts of housemovers as much as the news that the home of their dreams comes with a long chain attached.

  If you're in a chain, you're at the mercy of the most disorganized person with the most inefficient solicitor (of which more later). One person drops out and you're all back to square one while a substitute is found. Finally, so long after you first made the offer that you can hardly remember the property you're buying, the whole chain signs on the dotted line on the same day.

- The bits of paper solicitors need to gather together (to prove that the seller has a right to sell, that the house has seen a lick of paint in the last 20 years, that both sides can afford the homes they want and other tedious but necessary information) are all stored in different places and have to be found. Under the existing system, which has gradually evolved since we started becoming a nation of homeowners after World War I, no one starts organizing paperwork until after an offer has been made and accepted. This means an excruciating gap of several weeks while the seller's mortgage lender searches for title deeds, freeholders (if one or both the properties is leasehold) supply copies of invoices and service charge accounts and everyone searches frantically for pay slips or accounts to prove to their lenders that they're good for a loan. Meanwhile, the buyer's solicitor is contacting local authorities for searches, checking land registry records and sending out forms for the seller to complete in mind-boggling detail. All this means paper shuffling on a monumental scale.

All this means

paper shuffling

on a monumental scale

- Neither side is committed to anything until all the papers are shuffled and on the right desks. The longer the to-ing and fro-ing goes on, the more danger there is that the deal will fall through. According to the Department of Transport, Local Government and the Regions, the average property transaction in England and Wales takes eight weeks from when an offer is accepted to when contracts are exchanged and both sides are legally bound to the deal. It takes on average another four weeks after that to complete the sale and hand over the rest of the money. Other countries manage a similar process in half the time, with both sides signing binding contracts in as little as a week. Not surprisingly, the twin curses of gazumping, when a seller accepts a higher offer in a rising market, and gazundering, when a buyer reduces his offer in a falling market, are almost unknown in countries where both sides are legally bound to the deal at the start. By contrast many English and Welsh buyers have had the bitter experience of spending several thousand pounds in fees for surveys, local authority searches

The average property transaction

in England and Wales

takes eight weeks

from when an offer is accepted

to when contracts are exchanged

Gazumping and gazundering

are almost **unknown** in countries

where **both sides are legally bound**

to the deal at the start

and solicitors' costs only to find that their seller has accepted a higher offer and they are out of the loop and out of pocket, usually with no redress.

- Selling and buying property brings out the worst in otherwise reasonable people. Even if you all initially get on like a house on fire, sitting around over a civilized glass of wine discussing boiler repair contracts and damp proof courses, you will hate the very sound of each others' names several months down the line after a scorching row about whether the best dining room curtains are included in the price and why the buyer's solicitor keeps repeating questions about maintenance costs and boundary fences to which the seller claims he's already provided answers.

- Everyone blames everyone else for everything. There are a lot of people involved in property transactions, with plenty of scope for slip ups and communication breakdowns. Your solicitor will never admit

Everyone blames

everyone else

for everything

that a vital document has been lying in his secretary's in-tray for typing for several days (yes, this is how many solicitors still work, even in the internet and email age) and will instead blame the delays on the other side's solicitors/the local authority/the buyer's surveyors/someone else a couple of notches up or down the chain.

What all this means is that the hassle-free property transaction is the exception rather than the rule. But you can help yourself if you understand the rules of the game. This is where this book comes in:

- *If you're selling*. It will take you through the whole process of putting your property on the market at the right time in the market cycle, getting it valued and correctly priced so that you get a good offer. You will find out what to expect from an agent and how to choose a good one.

- *If you're buying*. You'll find out how to look at areas and properties critically, how to deal with agents and homeowners and why no one really knows if house prices are going up, down or sideways.

- *It will explain* what should be happening at every stage of the buying and selling process from when you make an offer to when you exchange contracts, explaining why you need to investigate the history of leasehold properties even more carefully than freehold homes and why a structural survey should be a necessary expense.

- *If you're buying a new home*. All the tricks of the trade are exposed, from the small touches which make a showhouse or flat look bigger than it really is, to the structural problems of new homes for which no one wants to take responsibility.

- *If you need a mortgage*. You will discover what all the words in mortgage advertisements mean, how to see through pushy endowment salesmen and how to choose a suitable loan.

- *If you're renting*. The whole process is explained from finding a property to signing the tenancy agreement. And if you fancy becoming a landlord, use the book to help you choose the right property, the right agent and the right tenant.

But the book won't just tell you how to go out tomorrow and buy, sell or rent a house. Integral to every chapter is an analysis of the impact the internet is having on the various sectors of the property market and explanations of how you can use the net to help you take control of the housebuying process, along with hundreds of useful web addresses and reviews of major sites. You will find out:

- how the internet is changing the way we househunt

- how useful (or not) major property websites are for finding your ideal home and what the limitations of the internet are as a househunting/house-selling tool

- how you can use the internet to download vast tracts of useful information about local areas, local councils, schools, transport links and future plans for places you're considering living in

- if it's really true that you can get a better mortgage deal over the internet

- why you should be expecting solicitors to speed up their act over the next few years

- why you may never need to sign on the dotted line of a property or mortgage contract again.

....

Caveat

Internet sites come and go very quickly. All the sites reviewed and/or listed in this book were checked out and all existed at the time of going to print. But there's no guarantee that sites will still be up and running by the time you read this book. If a site has closed or merged, you may be automatically switched to another one. If not, use search engines such as Yahoo! **www.yahoo.co.uk** (used for most of the research in this book),

Ask Jeeves (at **www.ask.co.uk**) or AltaVista (at **www.altavista.com**), which often scored where Yahoo! failed.   *Google ?*

Online security and privacy

Using the internet to search for properties or mortgages often means registering in order to use all the facilities of sites. The most usual pieces of information you will be asked to supply are:

- your name, address and phone number

- your email address

- details of your income and credit history if you're getting mortgage quotations online.

Before you supply this information click on the site's 'terms and conditions' or 'privacy' pages for an explanation of what they will do with this information. Look for a promise that personal information supplied by you won't be passed on to third parties without your permission. You should be able to opt not to receive unsolicited marketing emails by ticking or unticking a box.

The Office of Fair Trading (**www.oft.gov.uk**) has an excellent and detailed section on its site full of useful tips if you do buy anything online. The OFT issues the following advice:

- Don't be taken in by a snappy-looking website. Sites can pop up and disappear again just as quickly.

- Check out the company's track record. Do you know someone else who has successfully used the company? Don't always believe onsite testimonials from 'happy customers' – these can be easily faked.

- Check the company's privacy statement.

- Look at the web address and check the company is physically in the UK (just because its address ends in .co.uk, doesn't mean it's

It's difficult

to get your money back

from companies outside

the jurisdiction of the UK courts

physically in the UK). It's difficult to get your money back from companies outside the jurisdiction of the UK courts.

- ● Look for traders which have an encryption facility to scramble your card details while they're in transit. Safe sites will display a padlock at the bottom of the payment screen.

- ● For investments (equities, endowments, pensions for example), check with the Financial Services Authority (**www.fsa.gov.uk**) that a company is registered. It's a criminal offence to sell investments without being authorized and you won't be eligible for compensation if the firm collapses taking your money with it. Call the Financial Services Authority's public enquiries office (0845 606 1234) to check authorization.

- ● Look for traders signed up to codes of practice, such as TrustUK **www.trust.org.uk**, a government-sponsored organization. Sites showing the TrustUK hallmark will protect your privacy; make sure your payments are secure; confirm what you've bought and let you cancel; deliver goods and services within an agreed time period and sort out complaints.

- ● Under the Consumer Protection (Distance Selling) Regulations, you have special rights when buying over the net. These include receiving clear information before placing an order; written information about purchase; a cooling-off period in which you can cancel your order without reason and get a full refund; and a full refund if you don't get the goods ordered by an agreed date or within 30 days of placing the order.

Check your credit rating & get it disentangled from IVB's :-
Experian 0115-934 4050
www. experian. co. uk
Equifax 0870· 010 0583
www. equifax. co. uk

1

BUYING

BY THE END OF THIS CHAPTER YOU WILL

....

- Know how to tell an up and coming area from one that's down and going

....

- Understand why it's vital to lurk on street corners late at night while househunting

....

- Start to have a sneaking sympathy for New Labour's league table performance obsession

....

Where do you start?

'With the money' is the short answer. Going shopping for a mortgage is a lot less fun than spending a delicious voyeuristic weekend househunting and if you're in the enviable position of not needing to sell your existing home to buy another and not needing a loan, skip to the next section. But if in common with most people you can't lay your hands on a spare few hundred thousand pounds, you need to know how much you can borrow and what sort of home you can aspire to. If you're selling, get a valuation on your existing home (see Chapter 2), then check out mortgage deals. There's a dizzying choice of mortgage lenders, types of loan and ways of shopping for funds, all of which are dealt with in detail in Chapter 4. What you should end up with after a trawl along the high street, a surf across the net or a visit to a mortgage broker, is the promise of a mortgage in principle. No lender will go firm on a mortgage offer until you've found a property which can be valued for mortgage purposes but a mortgage in principle means that a lender is satisfied you can afford the repayments. Expect to have to produce payslips, or accounts if you're self-employed, and to have your creditworthiness checked (this is now the work of a moment as lenders' systems get increasingly sophisticated). Once you've got a mortgage in principle, sellers and estate agents will take you more seriously than someone who has just wandered in from the street wondering vaguely if there are any properties for sale.

What you should end up with is the promise of a mortgage in principle

Househunting is

a serious business

so be prepared to

put in the time

Starting your search

Be focused. That is the sensible advice from one agent. This may seem obvious but agents complain that many buyers haven't got a clue where they want to live and just hope something will turn up. Remind yourself that you are about to make the biggest purchase of your life and will have to live with, as well as in, the consequences if you make the wrong decision. Househunting is a serious business so be prepared to put in the time.

Get the area lowdown

Statistically, you're more likely to move a couple of miles down the road than to a part of the country you've never been to before. But, especially in cities, just crossing the street can thrust you into a different milieu, as rich and poor exist cheek by jowl and it's not unusual for million-pound penthouses to overlook council flats. Even if you think you know an area quite well you may be surprised when you start serious research.

You'll save time and have a better chance of finding somewhere you actually like at a price you can afford if you've done some ground work before falling in love with the first property you see.

TOP TIPS

- *Be realistic.* If you know how much you can spend, as you should by this stage, there's no point drooling over a chic little mews house or divine old rectory in rolling acres when you know you'll end up with a two up, two down terrace or a Victorian conversion flat with a cupboard as a second bedroom.

- *Be specific.* Do you want a flat or a house? Do you long for a trendy city-centre loft or is your idea of bliss a suburban semi with offstreet parking for the lawnmower? Do you want period or modern?

- There's no substitute for putting your walking boots on and actually exploring areas you're interested in. Information sources such as the internet are a good start for gathering factual information on everything from types of property stock to how likely residents in a certain postcode are to drink gin or eat bacon sandwiches for breakfast (see Web Watch). But the only way to find out if they're also the sort of people who like to spend weekends taking their cars apart in the front garden is to go there.

- If you will need to use public transport, either because you don't have a car or because you need to commute, test out the journey by travelling to an area for the first time by whatever means of transport you plan to use. How long does it take? Is the station convenient for the centre of town/for roads that you're interested in?

- Even if you do have a car, get out and walk once you get there. This is a useful way of checking how easy it is to park, whether you'll need a parking permit and whether the street becomes an unofficial car park during shopping hours or in the evening. And walking means you can peer over fences and walls (does the railway run along the back? does the back garden of that beautiful looking house back onto a factory?), note down names and numbers of estate agents from sale boards, watch people going in and out of their houses and generally *be nosy*.

- Walk down the main street. Does it look prosperous or are there a lot of empty shops to let? How heavy is the traffic and are there any obvious rat runs? Does it feel safe and friendly? Do the streets look cared for or is there litter and graffiti?

- Simple things like buying local newspapers will give you a feel for the tone of the area and what the burning issues are (letters pages are especially useful). Talk to friends who live in the area or tune in to conversations in shop queues.

- Check intangibles which could influence your choice – school league tables, crime rates, how efficient the local council is. The current government's obsession with league tables and targets has resulted in an explosion of data on everything from how quickly phones are answered at the town hall to how many rubbish collections the council misses. All this information should be available in local libraries, through the town hall or on the internet.

WEB WATCH

➡ **Council sites.** Most councils have their own websites. Quality varies but the sensible ones have made an effort. You'll glean a feel for the area – a potted history, future plans, council priorities. Look beyond the inevitable upbeat and optimistic tone for facts. For example, every council now has to produce an annual report on its performance compared with other councils and there should be at least a summary of the report on the site. Try clicking on Performance or Best Value (a reference to recent laws compelling councils to demonstrate they are providing best value). **www.lganet.gov.uk**, the website of the Local Government Association, contains the web addresses of every local authority in England and Wales. For Scottish local authority web addresses go to the Confederation of Scottish Local Authorities (COSLA) at **www.cosla.gov.uk**.

➡ **Government sites.** Useful sites if you're moving to a new area include the Department for Education and Skills (**www.dfes.gov.uk**) which has complete lists of school performance tables and a link to the Office for Standards in Education (OFSTED) at **www.ofsted.gov.uk**, for reports on individual schools. A brilliant site with links to loads of useful government and public sector bodies is **www.ukonline.gov.uk**. If you're moving house, check out the Life Episodes section, which includes Moving House (among other stressful life experiences like death, bereavement and dealing with crime). Under sections which include Searching for Property, Planning the Move, Making the Move and After the Move (for more on the last three see Chapter 6), there are links to information on everything from transport and schools to jobs and the environment in areas you're interested in. If you're worried about possible hidden nasties like pollution or contaminated land log onto **www.environment-agency.gov.uk** and click on What's In My Backyard? You can search by whole country, place name, postcode or grid reference and zoom in and out of detailed maps to check information on river quality, flood plains and pollution.

➡ **Other sites include:**

➡**www.upmystreet.com**

Background: Launched in 1998. One of the first to hit on the 'find out what's in your area' formula, now much copied.

How it works: A mine of information on everything from schools, crime rates and council tax to local pubs, restaurants and late-night chemists, all specific to your postcode. Key in your postcode (a full postcode gets the best results) or town and call up a massive database of statistics and lists from an impressive range of sources including the Land Registry (property prices), the

Audit Commission (council performance), Thompsons Local Directories (services), the Good Food Guide (restaurants), the Education Department (school league tables) and the police (crime figures). There's an intriguing section on the socio-economic and demographic makeup of your postcode area. Click on About the Data at the top of each section for explanations of the figures.

Pros: Slick and easy to use with no unnecessary graphics. Lots of links to other sites including local estate agents, solicitors, surveyors and mortgage providers. Solidly factual and much improved since the early days in 1998 when it carried some outdated information.

Cons: Can be slow to load.

Verdict: A high profile site, much quoted in the media. A must even if you think you know an area well. And quicker than going to the library.

➡ **www.yell.com**

Background: Online site of Yell, formerly the Yellow Pages.

Claim: Features around 1.7 million UK classified business and services listings plus local one-stop shop listings including a comprehensive property section.

How it works: You can search by postcode for property for sale (the site is linked with **www.assertahome.co.uk**, see later), financial advice and neighbourhood information including schools, council tax and house prices. You can also find out if your new property is in a high clay subsidence area or at risk from radon gas by using the HomeSight property search service from information giant Equifax. You can order postcode-specific reports online, at a cost of £24 for radon and £26 for clay subsidence, which will be delivered in three working days. The site also links to **www.ihavemoved.com**, which provides free change of address services for when you've managed to move (see Chapter 6).

Pros: Lots of useful links, easy to navigate and quick to load.

Cons: Some out-of-date information. House prices are sourced from the Land

Registry but the site didn't carry the latest quarter's figures. Log onto **www.landreg.gov.uk** for the most up-to-date figures in your area.

➡www.homecheckuk.com

Background: Part of Bridge Security, commercial security specialists, established 1995.

Claim: Private investigators carry out surveillance checks to alert you to potential problems at your new home, including noisy neighbours, traffic, flight paths, pollution and inefficient rubbish collections.

How it works: You pay an average of £300 for an investigator to quiz your prospective neighbours and generally case the joint. Get a confidential report delivered in seven days.

Pros: Fast to load; uncluttered pages.

Cons: Wordy and sometimes ungrammatical text which reads like the contents of PC Plod's notebook ('Ensuring you peace of mind by providing detailed reports of potential neighbours, noise and other factors important to you when choosing a new home'); limited links to other sites.

Verdict: Knock on a few doors, walk the streets at different times of day and save yourself £300.

➡www.ukpropertyguide.co.uk

Background: Part of UK Net Guides.

Claim: Gateway to a useful range of property-related websites, including information sites (house price indices, online maps and photos and how to find out if your dream home has subsidence or is affected by radon gas).

How it works: Provides lists of links to buying, selling, renting, buying at auction and buying direct, graded by star system, as well as sites for removal firms, schools and other property-related services. Partnered with Assertahome (see later) for property sales information.

Pros: Does some of the leg work for you.

Cons: Star rating system would be more useful if it was clear what criteria were being used.

➡ www.thisislondon.co.uk

Background: Formerly **www.underoneroof.com** and now rebranded as part of the *London Evening Standard*'s this is London website.

Claim: 39,359 properties on the site throughout London and the south east.

How it works: You can search for properties for sale or to rent by inputting the first part of your postcode. The search brings up brief details and photos and you can bring up further details, link to the agent's site or send an email. Local information, accessed by borough then broken down into area, is based on the *Evening Standard*'s successful *Where to Live in London* guide (written by yours truly). Property news links you to the most recent issue of the *Evening Standard*'s Wednesday homes and property section.

Pros: The quick search panel is accessible throughout so you don't have to go back to the beginning if you want to start a new search.

Cons: Limited number of agents appear to be signed up.

➡ Other sites worth checking out, especially if you're looking for links to other sites or want to catch up on property news, include **www.findaproperty.com** (an excellent source of links to other sites listed under themed headings including architecture and building, buying and letting, plus interesting property news and features) and **www.0800homes.co.uk**.

➡ For an update on who owns which sites, what's merged with what and which sites agents consider the best in terms of properties, features and appearance, go to **www.reapit.com**. The site, primarily aimed at estate agents, ranks property portal sites, with comments and reviews about each one.

How to spot an up and coming area

Some areas have always been up – the affluent parts of the Home Counties such as Buckinghamshire and Surrey, smart parts of central

London such as Belgravia and picture postcard rural retreats like the Cotswolds spring to mind. But the Holy Grail of homeownership for many is to buy a rundown property somewhere shabby and unfashionable, only to see prices rocket as the area gentrifies and becomes the last word in trendiness. Cities are especially prone to such shifts. Patterns of employment change, leaving empty factories, warehouses and offices ripe for conversion. New transport links open, bringing previously farflung areas within commuting distance. And big price rises in established places force people further afield to colonize neighbouring areas, which in turn become gentrified as people with money move in and are able to sustain a local economy of shops and restaurants.

Thirty years ago Islington in north London and Fulham in west London were shabby working-class areas, beyond the pale for the middle classes. Now prices there are astronomical. Fulham's rise, in the late 1980s, was due to its proximity to desirable Chelsea. Islington was close to central London with some wonderful Georgian townhouses ripe for restoration. Other city centres (Bristol, Leeds, Manchester, Cardiff) have seen a renaissance as developers move in to restore and rebuild along urban waterways and around dock basins.

So what makes an area ripe for gentrification? Yolande Barnes, head of research at FPD Savills, suggests watching out for the following:

- *Good existing transport links or plans for new links.* Areas are often cheap because they're difficult to get to. The arrival of new lines or even markedly better services (turn up and ride tube-style services instead of timetabled train services for example) jacks up prices instantly. In London, where it can take a couple of hours to travel from one side to the other, people will pay up to 20 per cent more for properties near tube or Docklands Light Railway stations. (Tubes are much more popular than trains, which are widely perceived as slow and infrequent, with the added inconvenience of having to change at a

London terminus.) And once transport connections are in place, the whole surrounding area starts to take off, as in areas of south east London like Bermondsey or Rotherhithe, newly connected to the tube system by the Jubilee Line. Keep an eye on planned new links in the worst served south east and north east via the website of the Greater London Authority **www.london.gov.uk**. Local authority websites around the country will have details of regeneration plans in their own areas.

- *A good stock of period property, preferably Georgian or Victorian.* After a fall off in popularity in the 1960s and 1970s, period styles came back into favour with a vengeance and have been hot favourites with the buying public ever since. Original features such as cornicing, fireplaces, tiles, stained glass and dado rails can push up prices substantially. The bigger the house is the better, as it can be converted into generous high ceilinged flats or restored to a family home. By contrast, suburban 1920s and 1930s semis, built to a more modest scale, don't convert well and suburbs generally have yet to experience the revival of the inner city, especially among the young and affluent.

- *Places close to existing established areas.* This will reduce the risk that you will be left high and dry in a rundown dump. Higher prices in *eg Crouch End* neighbouring areas will force people to turn to the closest affordable options. The key to gentrification is critical mass, which will then attract all the wine bars, little boutiques and designer clothes shops serving the affluent.

Original features such as

cornicing, fireplaces, tiles, stained glass and dado rails

can push up prices substantially

- *Early signs of middle-class habitation.* In the high street, this can mean a café or restaurant serving bruschetta and rocket salad rather than egg, bacon, tea and two slices (although as Yolande Barnes points out, the time to cash in on the opening of such establishments is when the old is still boarded up, poised for the arrival of the new). Estate agents and developers are another sign of gentrification – they tend to follow the money and react to trends, albeit quickly in the case of developers who don't want to pay more than they have to for land.

- *Telltale signs of the beginning of a middle-class takeover in residential streets.* (If all the houses in a street already bear the signs, you're too late.) These include wooden slatted blinds rather than net curtains at the windows, bookshelves rather than a huge widescreen TV and an England flag, skips in the street, tidy front gardens and careful restoration of original front doors and windows rather than evidence that the double glazing man has clocked up another sale.

How to deal with estate agents

The world is full of estate agents. See an empty shop in a high street and the chances are its windows will soon be full of property details while eager young men and women in shirt sleeves seize telephones or try to look busy going through their appointment books. Their magazine and newspaper advertising is responsible for the death of millions of trees, their boards spring up in every street and you can download details of properties across the world from glossy websites. Most estate agents will be charming, friendly and accommodating. After all, they want you to buy a property from them.

The world is
full
of estate agents

But never forget:

1 An estate agent works for the seller, not for you. He's being charming because he wants to tie up a deal which will net him commission from the seller.

2 If a rival buyer comes along with a better offer, you have no legal protection. Agents legally have to pass on all offers and if this means you lose out to someone prepared to pay more, tough.

You don't have to buy your home through an estate agent. Properties for sale privately are advertised everywhere from local newspapers to the internet and you can negotiate direct with the owner, who almost certainly knows more about his property than any agent ever could.

But never forget:

1 Good estate agents know the market, what's for sale and what's coming up. Play your cards right and you could be first into properties that no one else even knows are for sale.

2 You will have access to a much wider range of properties through agents, who sell the vast majority of properties in England and Wales. Scotland is different (see Chapter 3).

How to get the best out of an agent

- Pick out agents who appear to have a wide selection of properties like the one you're looking for. If you're buying locally, you may have a good idea anyway from talking to friends, keeping an eye on agents' windows or spotting whose noticeboards go up on which properties. Agents who appear to have cornered the market in rundown semis next to dual carriageways aren't likely to have the clout or the price knowledge to sell secluded mansions on the neighbouring private estate.

- If you're not local, a good starting point is to use property search engines on sites which carry properties from a range of agents (see Web Watch). Typing in the name of an area, or postcode if you know it, the type of property you're after and the number of bedrooms will give you an idea of agents and prices. You should be able to download full details and photographs and email for an appointment to view. But most property sites, even the major ones, only give a limited picture. It depends how many agents are signed up, what markets they're serving and how assiduous they are in keeping their property details up to date.

- However you make contact initially, try and set out your requirements specifically enough to avoid being sent all the dross that's been at the back of the filing cabinet for the past six months, without being so inflexible that you shut yourself off from interesting possibilities. Decide what you can't do without – a certain number of bedrooms, a garden, a certain grid of streets near good shops or schools – and what you will compromise on – maybe the sitting room doesn't have to be south facing or you could bear to live with offstreet parking rather than a garage.

- Register with several agents and get on their mailing lists. It costs nothing, there's no obligation and you'll get details of more properties.

- Keep in contact. In a booming market, there's likely to be a shortage of property and you'll only get what you want if you imprint yourself on the agent's brain as a serious buyer. This means ringing in every few days to check what's just come on and being ready to view likely prospects quickly. If the agent you're using has a service which automatically emails you with details of good property prospects when you've registered, use it and act on it. Estate agents are only human and like anyone else, they'll react positively if you look keen.

DID YOU KNOW?

Most agents keep private notes, on card indexes or computers, of buyers, categorizing them as HOT (hot prospects), particularly if they have NTS (nothing to sell). If you're HOT with NTS, expect a warm welcome, especially if you're an FTB (first time buyer). Not only do you have NTS but you'll help hoover up the starter homes and small conversion flats at the bottom of the market, helping their owners to move up to the next rung on the property ladder. And if you have saved up a substantial deposit (15 per cent or more of the property's price) and don't have to go cap in hand to a mortgage lender for a 100 per cent loan, your estate agent will be positively ecstatic.

WEB WATCH

➡ www.rightmove.co.uk

Background: One of the largest aggregate property sites, jointly owned by Countrywide Assured Group, the financial services group, the Halifax, Royal & Sun Alliance and Connell.

Claim: 4000 corporate and independent agents signed up, representing more than 167,000 properties and covering 99 per cent of UK postcodes. Of the top (biggest) 100 agents, responsible for 95 per cent of house moves, rightmove claims to have 55. Claims to have significantly more 'page impressions' (i.e. number of pages looked at, indicating activity) than any of its rivals. 'We have three and a half times more visitors every year than Alton Towers.'

How it works: Main function is as property search site. Search for property by name of area and/or postcode. Each property has a reference number, photo and brief description, although a recent magazine survey revealed that estate agents didn't always recognize the reference numbers of their own properties. Click on address of property for further details including room measurements. Plus useful pages on building terms, moving terms and legal stages in England, Wales and Scotland. Specializes in mass market and middle of the road property, not so hot on the upmarket stuff.

Pros: Easy-to-use site, easy to click back into search engine for multiple searches. Useful checklists for buying, selling and letting. Clear site, uncluttered with advertising, although arguably the overall visual effect is a bit old fashioned. Recent improvements include auto emailing, where you can arrange for potentially suitable properties to be emailed to you, and tighter area and distance definitions on the search engine.

Verdict: A good site, especially for standard suburban property.

➡ www.fish4.co.uk

Background: Launched in 1999. Owned by consortium of local newspaper groups. Heavily advertised on billboards, on online search engines like Ask and MSN and on TV by annoying people rushing around in fish costumes on motorbikes.

Claim: 176,148 properties available online for sale and rent. Updated daily.

How it works: Fish4 is essentially online classified advertising, with sections on jobs, homes, cars and other items you'd expect to find in the classified section of local papers. The property section allows searches by postcode or place name for sales and lettings and you can get the usual mix of service directories and local information. There's useful advice on buying a new home as well as an existing one, a 'jargon buster' and an estate agents' directory.

Pros: Home page sets out what's on the site comprehensively although the layout is a bit messy and there are the usual flashing advertising logos. Fast loading and easy to navigate.

Cons: Local information didn't seem very informative – lists of numbers of cinemas, restaurants, local services and so on within 10-minute drive of centre of any given postcode area without any further detail. Estate agents' directory wasn't specific enough to be useful.

Verdict: Strongest in mass and middle market properties in areas where its owners are strong. Not good for upmarket property.

➡ **www.assertahome.co.uk**

Background: Launched May 2000 by CGNU (the merged Commercial Union and Norwich Union insurance groups).

Claim: 'Designed to help you with the whole process of moving home from checking out the local amenities to settling in.'

How it works: Key in a postcode or place name and details of number of bedrooms, price range and type of property and you get brief details with a photo. Click on the photo for full details. You can save property details and email agents with properties you're interested in. There are also links to charcolonline, the site of reputable independent mortgage adviser John Charcol and upmystreet (see earlier) for area information. You can get quotes for conveyancing and a service directory includes solicitors, removal firms, gas and electric companies and surveyors (although inputting the name of a surveying firm known to have moved offices came up with an out-of-date address).

Pros: Comprehensive, easy to navigate, fast working.

Cons: Home page is a bit old fashioned and flashing ads are distracting. Claims the highest number of properties on the market at any one time but a survey earlier this year found that only 54 per cent of the properties advertised were actually available.

Verdict: Solid middle market site with lots of properties from CGNU-owned Your Move as well as good range of other agents. An estimated 80 per cent of properties are selling for £200,000 or less.

➡ www.propertyfinder.co.uk

Background: Launched in 1995. Started by managing property databases for upmarket agents like Knight Frank, FPD Savills and John D. Wood, then launched as standalone site. Helped out financially recently with injection of money from Hamptons, another upmarket agent.

Claim: About 15,000 people visit the site a day and properties generate 1000 email enquiries daily.

How it works: Home page has quick search facility by postcode, number of bedrooms and type of property. Search provides full details, a decent photograph, a location map and facilities for emailing agents. There's also a one-click location map, directories of selling agents, surveyors, solicitors and removal firms and useful guides for buyers and sellers.

Pros: Gets straight to the point with property search.

Cons: Have to start again from scratch if you want to adjust the search e.g. by putting in new postcode. ☺ *so note your spec to speed filling it in again*

➡ www.primelocation.co.uk

Background: Launched in 2000 by a consortium of estate agents dominated by upmarket London players. Deliberately sets out to be the site for expensive properties. Demands that agents exclusively use Primelocation, which has put off some.

Claim: 'The perfect place for the perfect place.' An estimated 800 agents are listed on the site, which is owned by 240 agents.

How it works: A slick home page offers clearly marked options for buying, selling, letting and moving. You search for properties by location, type of property, price range and number of bedrooms. You can get full details onscreen and email agents. A good feature is that you can change some of the search criteria (postcode for example) without starting from scratch. There are useful guides for buyers, buying at auction and other topics, as well as links to upmystreet and homecheck for area information and ihavemoved for moving information. The site is thoughtfully arranged so that the different sections contain search facilities and general information grouped together. Going to the neighbourhood information section will bring you upmystreet and a couple of features about how to live with your neighbours.

Pros: Clearly signposted, much improved from initial attempt.

Cons: Some sections slow to load.

Verdict: Getting a grip on the expensive end of the market. Don't bother to log on if you want fewer than four beds or want to spend less than £250,000 – the search engine won't go that low.

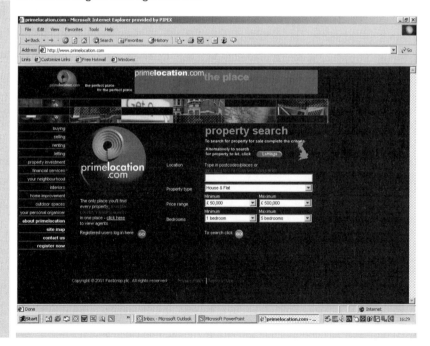

Prices are rising – no they're not

Once you've started thinking about buying a property, you will find your attention inexorably drawn to housing market reports regularly appearing in the national press and on television. The main producers of house price indices are:

- The Halifax **www.halifax.co.uk**. Now a bank (merged with the Bank of Scotland in 2001 under the name HBOS) and the UK's largest mortgage lender. Issues a monthly house price index and a more detailed quarterly regional commentary. Its strong presence in the north of England where property prices are lower results in generally more bearish house price indices and predictions than its rivals.

- The Nationwide **www.nationwide.co.uk**. The UK's largest remaining mutual building society. Issues monthly indices and quarterly regional commentaries coinciding regularly with the Halifax. More of a southern bias, which makes it more generally bullish than the Halifax.

- The Land Registry **www.landreg.org.uk**. Repository of details of every individual piece of registered land and property in the UK, including dates of when it changed hands and the price that was paid for it. Unlike the Halifax and the Nationwide indices, the Land Registry index includes cash purchases as well as properties bought with a mortgage. Issues quarterly figures for every local authority and London borough, breaking down sales into types of property (detached, semi-detached, terraced, flat/maisonette) with average prices paid in that authority for each type. Unlike the Halifax and Nationwide, the Land Registry's prices aren't seasonally or regionally adjusted. They are just raw averages. A couple of sales of expensive detached houses can lead to a major distortion in the figures. Likewise, in some areas too few of a certain type of house have changed hands to be able to get a coherent price picture.

The results of all these indices make great headlines but the sad truth is that they often as not contradict each other, confusing rather than clarifying. The figures are also only a rough guide to the real picture because they are averaged out over wide geographical areas, smoothing out huge variations within different parts of the country.

Viewing properties

This is arguably the best bit of the housebuying process. Indeed, some people enjoy having a good nose round so much that they go and view properties they have no intention of buying. But serious househunting, when you're desperate to find something you can imagine living in, can be physically exhausting and emotionally stressful. Good forward planning is vital. By this stage, you should have narrowed down your choice of areas and type of property. Viewing places you don't really want to live in/can't afford is a waste of everyone's time.

Clear your diary, preferably on a weekday when estate agents are less busy, and make appointments in advance to view a series of properties. This gives agents time to contact sellers if they don't hold keys or to organize keys if they do. Depending on how near likely prospects are to each other and which agents they are on with, you should be able to view three or four properties in an afternoon, especially if an agent has block booked time out of the office and takes you by car.

Some people **enjoy having a good nose** round **so much that they go** and view properties they have **no intention of buying**

When you view

Think location

Estate agents who actually come out with the cliché of 'location, location, location' in front of you risk looking pretty naff. But location can make a huge difference, not only to the price you pay but also to how easy the property will be to resell. However much you play around with furniture, wall coverings and interiors, you can't alter a bad location. Watch for the following locational downsides:

- *Busy roads*. Can be a big turnoff (in the emotional, property-searching sense) particularly if a house is near a busy junction where there's constant starting and stopping of cars and lorries changing into low gear and revving up. The more upmarket the property, the trickier it is to sell.

- *Railways*. A small pootling branch line without too many trains can be quite soothing. But a busy inter-city line with hundreds of trains roaring past at 100 miles an hour is another matter, as is a line with lots of freight movement. Check train timetables and ask train companies about freight movements.

- *Pylons/electricity substations/mobile phone masts*. Offputting to many people, both because they look ugly and because of potential health problems, particularly for children. A pylon in sight of a property can devalue it by up to 15 per cent, while actually having one in the garden can take 40 per cent off the price and double the time it takes to sell.

- *Pubs/schools*. It may sound like the stuff of dreams to have a pub next door if you're a sociable type but you may regret it if it attracts drunken yobs and Saturday night fights under your window are a weekly occurrence. Similarly, a school could be great if you've got children of the right age and the school has a good reputation but breaktimes can be a noisy distraction if you work from home.

- *Footpaths/shared drives*. Shared drives or access can be a major source of tension between neighbours, sometimes escalating into headline-grabbing court battles. Check exactly who has a right to do what if you've very keen on the property otherwise. Footpaths and rights of way right under your window or across your garden can also feel like an invasion of privacy so check exactly where they run on an Ordnance Survey map to avoid disputes. Even if you don't mind ramblers striding across the lawn while you're eating your Sunday lunch, others might. Footpaths right next to your house can devalue it by up to 15 per cent.

Think property

- *Make notes as you go round*. After seeing several properties in a row, they'll start merging together in your mind. You don't have to write a thesis on each one – short notes such as 'small kitchen', 'would need new bathroom' or 'well stocked garden with pond' are probably enough to jog your memory.

- *Try not to be too influenced by existing décor or furniture*. Décor can be changed and furniture won't be there if you move in, but such leaps of imaginations are often tricky. According to pyschologist Dr Barrie Gunter, we all respond subsconsciously to the messages a property gives out. Contents of front rooms invitingly on display? The message is that the owner is sociable and approachable. Open-plan sitting/dining room? Great if you love entertaining. Tastes in books, kitchen equipment, pictures similar to yours? You love it immediately. Hate the décor but can imagine ripping it all out and starting again? You still want it because you know you will be able to imprint your personality on it.

- *Check boring but necessary things that would cost a lot to repair or replace*. Open the airing cupboard – does the boiler look recent? Ask to see the fusebox (speaking from personal experience, you may get some odd looks but, believe me, it's worth it). If it looks like a prop from the BBC's World War II epic cupboard, then the whole house could need rewiring, especially if light switches and flexes look old. Check the condition of roof tiles, down pipes and guttering as well. All this should be covered in your survey (see Chapter 3) but it doesn't take an expert to see if the tiles are falling off the roof. If you can't see from the outside, climb into the loft if it's accessible and check for daylight coming in through gaps in the tiles.

- *Revisit properties you're serious about at different times of day* so that you can check when certain rooms are likely to be darker and whether the street feels as safe and quiet at nine o'clock at night as it does at midday.

Think owner

It pays to be pleasant to the owner if he or she is there when you view. If it comes to a bidding war in a boom market and you've hit it off with the owner, you could seal the deal even if you haven't offered the highest price (see Making an offer). During the course of a pleasant initial conversation, ascertain the following:

- *Why are they moving?* This give you an idea of likely timescales and how serious they are. Job moves, needing to trade up to a larger home with a growing family, trading down because of a divorce are all good reasons to move. The less specific they are, the more suspicious you should be. Under the current housebuying system, it costs people nothing to put their home on the market experimentally just to see if there are any takers and they may take it off the market just as casually. (A proposed requirement to provide a seller's pack before marketing a property at a cost of around £500 should help discourage such cavalier behaviour. See Chapter 2.) Caginess may also indicate problems with noisy neighbours or disputes with freeholders in leasehold properties.

Sellers legally have to declare problems or disputes as part of the conveyancing process (see Chapter 3) but only if they've had cause to make a formal complaint. So if the neighbours have wild parties with loud music every night or the freeholder brings in cowboy builders to carry out repairs, the owners may be desperate to sell up and escape rather than complain.

- *Have they found somewhere to move to?* A vital question, to be asked straightaway. Ideally, the reply should be that they can be as flexible as you want, move into rented accommodation, stay with relatives or anything as long as they're prepared to exchange contracts quickly. If they've found somewhere to move to without too long a chain, that's also good news. But if they haven't found anywhere, be prepared for disappointment, or at best a long wait. Hundreds of sales a year fall through because sellers haven't found somewhere to move to.

- *How long have they lived there?* Most sellers imagine that the longer they have lived in a property, the more reassuring it will be for buyers. Up to a point. It probably means life there is at least tolerable. But people who have lived in one place for a long time have probably also got used to idiosyncracies and imperfections like non-existent or inefficient central heating, draughts, badly laid out kitchens with no work surfaces or a lack of bathrooms, which can be expensive to put right. If they're moving after only a couple of years, are they DIY enthusiasts or doers up of property who have watched too many episodes of 'Changing Rooms' and are doing a runner before the whole house collapses round their ears? A structural survey (see Chapter 3) should unearth any evil secrets.

- *What work have they had done?* If the reply is 'my brother's a builder and he extended the loft a couple of years ago', this could be a bad sign that corners have been cut, walls taken out where they shouldn't have been and changes made to the property without proper consents or planning permission (see Chapter 6). Equally, everything could all be above board. But don't leave anything to chance. Make sure your solicitor checks consents and permissions.

- *What fixtures and fittings are they leaving?* This will be decided in detail later on during the conveyancing process (see Chapter 3). But it's worth finding out roughly what is included in the price. It's convenient if washing machines, dishwashers, cookers and other white goods are left and plumbed in, saving you having to buy immediate replacements or have the hassle of bringing yours from your existing property.

DID YOU KNOW?

Buying Agents

If you don't have time to do your own househunting, one solution is a buying agent. Unlike an estate agent, who works for the seller, a buying agent works for you, the buyer. A number of upmarket estate agents including Knight Frank (**www.knightfrank.com**) and FPD Savills (**www.fpdsavills.co.uk**) have buying departments and a number of specialist companies like the Home Search Bureau (**www.homesearchbureau.com**) do nothing else. Having a buying agent is still very much a minority sport, restricted mainly to the wealthy with more money than time and it wouldn't suit those who love to househunt. But it can be a useful way of getting to the good properties before other buyers – buying agents market themselves on having such brilliant relationships with local estate agents that they're always first to hear of something that hasn't yet come onto the market. Expect to pay around 2 per cent of the price of the property in a buying agent's commission.

Having a buying agent is
still very much a minority sport

Making an offer

You find a place you love. You've been back several times and you still love it. You want to make an offer. How should you play it?

- If the market is booming, don't waste time offering anything below the asking price unless you know that the property has hung around a bit and the owner is getting desperate. (If the property has hung around, make sure you know why and can live with the reasons.)

- If the market is static, make an offer below the asking price. A good estate agent should be able to advise. Yes, they stand to make less commission if you pay less but they risk making no commission at all if you decide the price is too high and go elsewhere.

If you're in a strong position (finances arranged, offer for your property on the table), try getting the seller to agree to take the property off the market, at least for a certain number of weeks, to shut out potential gazumpers. You could ask him or her to sign a so-called lock-out agreement which gives you a clear run to work towards an exchange of contracts in, say, four weeks. If you fail to meet the target, the seller can remarket the property. Such agreements have long been championed by the National Association of Estate Agents, among others, but have never really taken off because of the volatility of housing markets in England and Wales, especially in London and the south east. In a rising market, sellers are reluctant to lose the chance of possibly getting more for their property and in a falling market they don't want to risk you getting cold feet and pulling out.

If the seller does agree to take the property off the market, make sure all agents know about this if more than one agent has been marketing it.

In a boom market, you may find yourself competing with several rival buyers for a property and you may be asked for 'sealed bids' or 'best and final offers'. These both amount to roughly the same thing – you submit your offer in writing by a certain deadline and the seller chooses which offer to accept. It need not be the highest. Sometimes it makes sense to accept a lower bid from a buyer who is in a stronger position to move quickly.

Making an offer is just the beginning. Neither side is committed to the deal for weeks or even months to come. Once an offer is made and accepted, all it signals is the firing of the starting pistol for the conveyancing process. However, if you are buying in Scotland, remember that a legally binding contract is made as soon as the seller accepts your offer.

2

SELLING

BY THE END OF THIS CHAPTER YOU WILL

- Know how to find out what your home is worth

- Be able to spot shark estate agents a mile off

- Know what your agent should be doing for his commission

- Understand why it's worth getting your property advertised on the internet

Selling and buying are covered in separate chapters in this book because each has its own set of rules and responsibilities. In practice, you'll probably be a seller as well as a buyer, using the proceeds from your existing property to buy another one. You'll find this creates a bizarre internal conflict. As a seller yourself, you can understand absolutely why the person selling to you is insisting that you take on trust his claim that maintenance costs are minimal (after all you've just done the same to the people buying your home) and the next minute, you're ringing your solicitor demanding minute details of all work done in the last 20 years to the property you're buying.

How to choose an estate agent

Most sellers don't have the time or the inclination to spend their spare time marketing their properties, showing potential buyers around, juggling offers and chasing solicitors to push the sale through. This is what estate agents are meant to do. Unfortunately, they don't all do it. Despite years of campaigning from consumer groups, estate agents still don't need to be licensed or professionally qualified and anyone can set up as an agent with no questions asked. Many firms have a high turnover of inexperienced staff under pressure to achieve quick sales at high prices, who lose interest as soon as you get an offer and the conveyancing process starts.

TOP TIPS

1   Look for the letters NAEA (National Association of Estate Agents) **www.naea.org.uk** or RICS (Royal Institution of Chartered Surveyors) **www.rics.org.uk** on letterheads, shop doors or websites. Both bodies set certain standards for members including requirements to pass professional exams (RICS) and have disciplinary and complaints procedures. A minority of agents who are members of RICS or NAEA are also members of the Estate Agents Ombudsman Scheme (**www.oea.co.uk**)

which has the power to investigate complaints and award compensation of up to £25,000.

....

2 Choose a firm which has properties similar to yours on its books. Such firms are more likely to have suitable buyers and be able to value your home accurately (see How much is your home worth?).

....

3 Go for firms with strong marketing skills. This doesn't have to mean glossy brochures (although these could be worth it for an expensive property). The least you should expect is a good photograph of your property attached to clear details. Go for firms with well laid out window displays (avoid curling fading photographs) and regular eye-catching advertisements in the local press.

....

4 Log on to the websites of prospective firms. Are the sites attractive and easy to use? And, vitally, do they carry up-to-date properties? Buyers soon learn to ignore sites where most of the properties have been withdrawn or sold. A firm with no website? Avoid it. In a recent survey more than half of respondents planning to move in the next 12 months would use the internet to search for a new home and you want your home to be up there on the web to give it maximum marketing exposure.

....

5 Remember the estate agent is working for *you*. Choose someone you get on with, who you can imagine talking to regularly on the telephone every few days for the next few weeks.

....

6 Narrow down your choice to two or three firms and ask them to come and value your property.

....

How much is your home worth?

The real answer, as honest estate agents will admit, is that your home is worth what someone else is prepared to pay for it. And this in turn depends on the state of the property market when you want to sell, where the property is and what other properties like yours are on the market or have recently been sold. Alongside the well-known estate agent's cliché of 'location, location, location' (i.e. it doesn't matter if it's a damp basement with no natural light as long as it's in Chelsea), it pays to remember another agent's mantra: 'Valuation is an art not a science.' In other words, agents haven't the faintest idea what your home is worth, so they'll make it up and hope to hook a buyer at the highest price possible.

Estate agents work on what they call 'comparables'. Agents asked to come and value your home will check what similar properties are selling for in your area before they come. This gives a very rough idea and works fine if yours is just one of thousands of Victorian terraces or starter homes on a new estate. But it's not so good for original or unusual properties which by definition don't have many comparables. Even if you have a house in an area where most of the properties are flats, valuing could be a problem.

You're more likely to get an accurate valuation from someone who has recently sold at least some properties like yours. Agents specializing in Georgian mansions at several million pounds a throw won't be experts in

Your home is **worth**

what someone else is

prepared to pay for it

small one-bed Victorian conversion flats in need of an urgent makeover and vice versa. (This doesn't mean they won't try – estate agents are salesmen and getting properties onto their books is their lifeblood, so beware.) One experienced London agent recommends getting three firms, one mass market, one middle market and one upmarket, to get a good range of values.

What to expect from a valuation

Good agents will:

- come armed with examples of similar properties they've sold recently (double-check these are completed sales rather than just offers, which can go pear shaped at any time) to demonstrate the prices they've achieved.

- have enough knowledge of your area to take local pricing quirks into account. For example, one road is more sought after than another because it's further from the dodgy pub/trading estate/main road, or properties on one side of the road are 25 per cent more expensive than the other side because they overlook green space rather than a busy railway line.

- be able to justify the price they come up with, not only with reference to the two previous points but also to the state of the local property market. Expect informed answers to general questions. Is there a shortage of flats/houses/property generally? Roughly how many buyers do you have on your books for my sort of property? How long is it taking you to get offers on similar places? You'll probably have a fair idea of the answers if you've been thinking of putting your home on the market for a while but estate agents are at the sharp end and should be professional housing market watchers.

generalities, sweeping statements and boasts about massive prices obtained for properties, without concrete evidence

- apparent ignorance of local issues. If an agent doesn't know that your road is one of a sought-after handful in the catchment area of a good primary school or that the whole street turns into the suburban equivalent of the M4 as drivers use it as a rush hour rat run, make your excuses and ask the agent to leave.

WEB WATCH

➡ A website worth checking to get your own idea of what properties are selling for in your area is **www.hometrack.co.uk**. This site collects and number crunches price information from selected estate agents in postcode areas across the country. Hometrack claims its mystery shoppers have checked out 10,000 agents and selected the best 20 per cent (best meaning the most clued up and keen to participate) to supply monthly postcode-linked price information. Prices are currently available for London and the south east, the south west, Birmingham and the Midlands and the north of England. The advantage of this site is that it is more detailed than other indices, using postcodes instead of local authority or regional divisions. The index shows not only average prices achieved but also indicators of market activity such as numbers of new buyers registered, number of properties registered and number of viewings per property. A disadvantage of the index is that some of the recommended agents seem to be a strange choice – not that local and not major players, so likely not to be that knowledgeable.

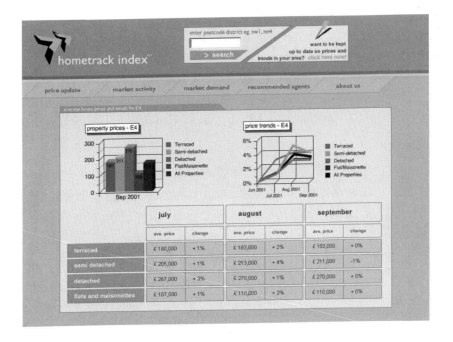

High, low or medium price?

Most agents will give you a verbal valuation on the spot, following up with a formal letter, which may also set out their terms of business and commission rates (see later). If they have to go away and think about how to price your property, this could be a bad sign, demonstrating lack of knowledge and/or homework. But equally, it could be because your home defies comparison.

What if there's a massive difference between the quotes? It can be very tempting to go with the agent who tells you his firm can easily get you £220,000, while others hover around the £200,000 mark. Before you choose, consider the following:

- *What is the market doing?* Is it booming with buyers fighting each other to make offers before agents have had time to draw up marketing details? If yes, you could strike lucky with a higher price. If no, your

All agents are **desperate**

for your business

but some are **more desperate** than others

home could hang heavy for months, getting more shop soiled as
buyers avoid it, thinking there's something wrong with it.

- *How quickly do you need to move?* If you aren't in a hurry, you can hold
  out for more money to spend on your next dream home (remembering
  that moving house is a costly business). If you need a quick sale and
  the market is just ticking along, marketing your home at a sharp price
  should shift it more quickly. But pricing it too low (assuming you can
  afford to take a lower price) can send out the wrong signal.

- *Are you asking a price which would incur a higher level of stamp duty for a
  buyer?* Stamp duty, which is calculated as a percentage of the sale price,
  is paid by the buyer and can be a heavy extra financial burden,
  especially on more expensive properties (see Chapter 3). If the price of
  your property would just push prospective buyers into a higher band,
  it may be sensible to lower the price and recoup the extra separately
  on fixtures and fittings, which don't attract stamp duty.

- *Is the agent desperate?* All agents are desperate for your business but
  some are more desperate than others, particularly if they're trying to
  get established or it's a national chain with exacting sales targets.
  Pitching a valuation high to win business may flatter your vanity and
  appeal to your inner greed but you may find your property sticking for
  several months before you're forced to concede and lower the price.

When to put your property on the market

There's no right time to sell. Many of us have no choice. Changes of job, family circumstances or financial difficulties can all mean a house move, maybe not at a good time. But if you do have any control over timing, these are the types of market you are likely to encounter:

- *Seller's market*. It's boomtime and you should get a quick sale at a good price. The downside is that if you are buying as well, you'll be paying top price for the property you buy and almost certainly fighting off rival buyers. This could be a case for taking the money and renting (see Chapter 7) until the froth comes off a bit.

- *Buyer's market*. As happened in the early 1990s, boom has turned to bust, house prices are dropping, sellers are desperate to trade their way out of trouble and there are precious few buyers on the horizon. Selling in this sort of market is hard work and buyers know they have you by the short and curlies. Small flats are particularly tricky to sell in this sort of climate because buyers can afford to leapfrog to larger properties, although investors buying to let will take the opportunity to hoover up some more stock. Bizarrely, the last recession saw agents' commissions rise although firms were going out of business left, right and centre. But if you're buying as well, you could get what, in retrospect, will look like a bargain.

- *Balanced market*. Rare in this small crowded island. In London and the south east, demand normally exceeds supply because this is where most of the jobs and the wealth are and building land is at a premium. In depressed parts of the north east, supply massively exceeds demand with whole streets of terraces selling for a couple of thousand pounds apiece or less.

There's no right time to sell

Remember housing markets are very local. Anything can affect them, from the closure of a major employer in the area to the payment of massive annual bonuses to City fat cats.

Agree terms

You're not legally obliged to sign a contract tying you to any specific agent (see Playing by the rules) but most agents will ask for some sort of commitment. Even if you're a bit commitment phobic, especially where estate agents are concerned, a written agreement should benefit you too in case of dispute later. Expect to be asked to agree one of the following:

Initially ● *Sole agency*. You give one agent the exclusive right to market your home for a set period of time. Most agents prefer this for obvious reasons and so do many sellers, believing (correctly) that it gives agents more incentive to get out there and make an effort. Four weeks is widely accepted as a fair period of time to give one agent free range, possibly a bit longer if the market is slow or your home is 'unusual' (a favourite estate agent's word, hinting at odd layout, outlandish décor or indeed almost anything that isn't a bog standard square box). Under a sole agency agreement, you aren't liable for the agent's commission if you sell to someone not introduced by the agent during the period of the sole agency. But you will have to pay up if your buyer had anything to do with your agent during the sole agency period, even if the sale goes through after the end of the period. You'll face two sets of commission if you have a sole agency agreement with one agent but sell your property through another during the period of the sole agency.

Avoid! ● *Sole selling rights*. Not the same as sole agency, so beware. A sole selling rights agreement means the agent can demand commission if your property is sold during the specified sole selling rights period, regardless of who sells it. In other words, if you or another agent do the work of finding a buyer, you still have to pay commission to the agent with sole selling rights, who has done precious little to earn the money.

- *Multiple agency*. Often used as plan B, after a property has sat around on the market for a while and plan A (get agent enthused with sole agency and home will sell in days) has failed. Under a multiple agency agreement, you put your home on with a number of agents and whoever sells the property gets all the commission. The downside for agents is that they don't have exclusive marketing rights and often multiple agency indicates a bit of desperation on the part of the seller – never a good selling point. The upside is that commissions are higher (see later) and winner takes all. From the seller's point of view, the property should get more exposure although you're paying more for it. But multiple agency can be offputting for buyers who are frightened that they could be gazumped by someone else introduced by another agent.

- *Joint sole agency*. Most frequently used for upmarket or unusual properties where a local and national agent get together for maximum marketing exposure, then split the commission.

How much do agents charge?

The amount of commission you'll have to pay depends on the type of agreement you have. Expect to pay around 1.75 per cent to 2 per cent of the sale price of your home for sole agency or sole selling rights and between 2.5 and 3 per cent for multiple agency or joint sole agency. But many agents are open to negotiation, particularly when they have a shortage of property on their books and think they can sell yours quickly at a good price. Some may agree to a flat fee, which can be a great deal for more expensive properties, although more expensive on cheaper ones. For example a flat fee of £2000 on a £200,000 property works out at 1 per cent excluding VAT. But £2000 on a £75,000 property works out at 2.6 per cent excluding VAT. VAT is payable on all commissions and fees at 17.5 per cent. Whatever deal you agree, make sure you understand the terms before you sign. Check what the commission includes. Will you get a good slot on the agent's internet site or any pooled property site on which the firm has a presence? Do they advertise in local papers? Do glossy brochures cost extra?

Selling your home on the internet

How important is the internet when you're selling your property? There's no doubt more and more people are getting hooked up to the internet, especially in London and the south east. In a MORI poll carried out on behalf of the Greater London Authority (GLA) at the beginning of 2001, 38 per cent of Londoners said they had access to the internet at home, more than a quarter used the internet for work or study and 35 per cent had an email address. Research on behalf of **www.rightmove.co.uk**, one of the largest online property sites, in March 2001 found that more than half of those planning to move house in the next 12 months planned to use the internet in their property search. Some central London agents estimate that half of those buying property through their offices come via the internet.

Estate agents are finally catching onto the new trend after a slow start when many of them feared they would be put out of business as sellers and buyers traded directly with each other on the web, cutting out the

Many sites **aren't technically** advanced because the agents concerned **can't bear to** relinquish control middleman. So far this hasn't happened to any great extent. The highest profile direct property selling site, **easier.co.uk**, collapsed earlier this year after blowing most of the £11 million it raised on the Alternative Investment Market on expensive advertising campaigns. It failed, according to commentators, because it didn't have enough properties on its website to offer buyers. It relied on homeowners posting details of their homes on the site and it didn't get critical mass.

And as agents and dot.com entrepreneurs alike have belatedly realized, what sellers want is for lots of buyers to visit sites on which their property is advertised and what buyers want is a good choice of properties in their price range to browse through. Obvious enough, you may think but you'd be surprised how many websites can't manage this much.

The online property buying scene is changing constantly, almost guaranteeing that the state of play will have altered by the time you read this. There's a lot of consolidation going on as sites backed by big banks and estate agencies expand by snapping up smaller sites which couldn't work out how to make their ventures pay once they had run out of start-up capital. Essentially, property websites fall into two main categories: estate agents' own websites and aggregated sites.

Estate agents' own websites

Almost all agents worth the name now have their own website. This is really an electronic shop window, where you should expect your property to be displayed, preferably with a good colour photograph and full sets of downloadable details. Buyers interested in your property should be able to email the agent directly to arrange a viewing. Also useful in making sure your property gets maximum exposure is a facility for buyers to register details of what they are looking for and receive regular electronic mailshots of potentially suitable properties. But many sites aren't this technically advanced, usually because the agents concerned are still ambivalent about the effect the net will have on their business and can't bear to relinquish control. This results in absurdities like having to ring up for full details to be posted or faxed, or having to ring to arrange a viewing, both of which could bug buyers. The so-called 'Walk Around Tour' is becoming a popular marketing tool for agents wanting to get your instruction and a number of agents have this facility on their sites. Instead of just seeing a single exterior or interior shot of a property, buyers can 'walk round' the whole house room by room on their screen via photographs taken with 360° fisheye lens cameras and even 'walk out' into the street. This can be useful for buyers who don't want to waste time viewing unsuitable properties although it's difficult to gauge the size of rooms correctly onscreen and the photographs, like any other taken for sales purposes, can be arranged to exclude inconvenient eyesores. Downloading details can also take a long time.

Aggregated sites

Nothing to do with sand or gravel but the industry name for sites or 'portals', displaying properties from a number of different agents. Keying words like 'property' into your search engine will bring up thousands of sites. But the dot.com downturn and the harsh economic realities of running a website are hitting online property sites just as hard as any other and sites which appear to be riding the storm best are those backed by corporate money from large estate agents or mortgage lenders. Some of the most well known are **www.assertahome.co.uk**, **www.rightmove.co.uk**, **www.fish4homes.co.uk**, **www.propertyfinder.co.uk**, and **www.primelocation.com**. These sites differ in design and ease of use but they work by asking buyers to key in a postcode or area and their requirements and producing information on homes from a number of agents active in the area. For buyers, this is (or should be) the electronic equivalent of walking down the high street and looking in lots of agents'

www.teamprop.co.uk (Prichett & Ellis)

windows. In practice, it can be a lot less useful. Numbers of agents can be limited as can types of property, depending on which agents have signed up. (See Chapter 1 for reviews of individual sites.) Some agents have deals with one site on which all their properties will appear exclusively – rightmove estimates that up to 30 per cent of the properties on its site won't appear anywhere else, for example, while other agents will appear on as many sites as they can. Most sites don't charge agents, making their money out of advertising or cross selling of mortgages instead.

Don't be overimpressed with sites which promise a 'unique service' or which claim to have cracked the secret of taking the stress out of housemoving. Buyers can have access to massive databases of information on local areas, buying, selling and moving tips, links to useful sites and so on but, as one chief executive of a large online property site comments, they still have to go through the same housebuying system as someone who's never logged onto the internet. And until the fundamentals change (as they look set to (see Chapter 3)), the stress will remain.

Fresh brewed coffee and home-baked bread?

What makes your home the one that buyers will fight over? The one that smells enticingly like the in-store bakery at Tesco's? Brewing up coffee and putting the half-bake supermarket bread in the oven as the doorbell rings are old marketing clichés. Who knows, they may still have the desired subliminal effect on some people. But more sensibly do:

- give window frames, doors and other visible exterior woodwork a lick of paint if the existing paintwork's looking a bit tired. First impressions count for a lot and often people will drive past and not even bother to go inside if they don't like the outside. Plane the front door so that it doesn't stick embarrassingly just when you're flinging it wide open with welcome.

What makes your home

the one that buyers will fight over?

- tidy up the garden, particularly the front, which people will see first. Cut the grass, weed the flowerbeds and clear out the cracks in the crazy paving.

- paint any rooms that desperately need it, especially the hall which is the first room buyers will enter.

- wash up, make the beds and tidy up before you go out each day. This can seem like a major hassle which gets worse the longer your home is on the market but people are easily put off by sinks full of dirty dishes, old food on kitchen surfaces and dripping washing hanging out all over the radiators.

- clear up the clutter and banish any rubbish you can't quite bring yourself to throw away to the attic or the back of the garage. Space is in and the bigger you can make your house look the better. Getting rid of surplus furniture also helps – if it isn't going to be surplus in your new home, find somewhere to store it until you've got a buyer.

Contrariwise, don't:

- spend a fortune redecorating the whole house, unless it so desperately needs it that it won't sell unless you do, in which case, stay neutral. Most buyers prefer to stamp their own individuality on their new home and very individual colour schemes could put people off.

- likewise, leave kitchens and bathrooms alone unless they're almost unusable or the only shabby bit in an otherwise expensive house. Given the choice, most buyers would prefer to pay less for the house and spend the money on upgrading with the kitchen and bathroom they want.

- install double glazing just to sell the property, unless it's in an area where double glazing is considered vital (near a main road for example). You probably won't recoup your outlay. But installing central heating is a different matter. People expect it and will pay more not to have the disruption of installing it themselves.

- convert an attic or loft into an extra room just to sell the house. You won't get your money back on the sale. Such alterations can be great ways to give yourself more space and save on moving costs but only do it if you intend to benefit from it yourself. See Chapter 6 for details of which home improvements add value and improve saleability.

WEB WATCH

➡ www.thefinaltouch.co.uk *Do they provide advice / Q&A on net?*

If your home isn't selling, call in the house doctors. A company called The Final Touch claims to be the first UK-based company to offer homeowners a complete facelift for their hard to shift homes. Services range from tactfully suggesting a clear-out of clutter to repainting the house in neutral colours. Co-founder Suzy Maas says most of her clients so far have been Londoners unwilling or unable to take their own properties in hand although the company boasts out-of-town clients too. An initial visit and report cost £150 for a one-bed property, £200 for a two-bed property, £250 for three beds and £300 for four beds. If you take on the company to do the work, the cost of the report will be deducted.

SELLERS' PACKS

As part of a pledge to reform the housebuying process in England and Wales, by common consent one of the slowest in the civilized world, the previous Labour government announced plans for a radical overhaul of the system. The centrepiece of the overhaul was the seller's pack. In a bid to cut the time it takes between accepting an offer and exchanging contracts binding both sides to the sale, it would be compulsory for sellers to put together packs of information on their properties before putting them on the market. The idea was that cutting the time between offer and exchange would reduce opportunities for gazumping, gazundering and the general messing around which can be so costly, emotionally as well as financially.

But the general election intervened and the Homes Bill, which included measures to introduce sellers' packs, was scuppered on its way through parliament. However, officials say the concept is still very much alive and kicking and will go through parliament again as soon as there's a slot in the legislative timetable. The original starting date for the introduction of the packs, the beginning of 2003, now looks unachievable but watch this space for revised dates.

The exact contents of the pack are still up for discussion and will be put in place through secondary legislation. But you (via your estate agent and/or solicitor) will almost certainly be expected to supply office copies of Land Registry documents proving you own the property; details of works carried out to the property with dates and costs; guarantees for treatments such as damp proofing or woodworm; copies of leases (for leasehold property); service charge accounts and management costs (leasehold properties); local authority searches and a survey of your property. These last two are proving the most controversial. Under the current system it is up to the buyer to instigate and pay for the search (see Chapter 3) and to commission a survey. Under the proposed system, the responsibility and cost will fall on the seller, who will be expected to pay an average of £560 to put together a pack.

Critics argue that most buyers will want to commission their own survey rather than rely on the seller's, despite changes in the law extending a surveyor's duty of care to the buyer so that the latter has a comeback. Whether this is true remains to be seen and ministers have so far stood firm on plans to require some sort of home condition report. But they are prepared to yield on another major sticking point – sellers of low value properties (as yet undefined) will be exempt from having to pay for sellers' packs.

Getting an offer

It's a great moment when you get an offer for your property. But play things carefully to get the best price. Here are the positions in which you could find yourself.

You get an offer for less than the asking price

If the market's looking sticky and you haven't had that much interest and/or your property is 'unusual'/needs lots of work, accepting may be the best option, especially if you suspect the asking price was a bit high in the first place. But if you think a buyer is just trying it on, it's your prerogative to hold out for more money. Offer to meet halfway if you think the buyer is in a strong position to go through with the sale – that is, he has an offer on his own property and has a mortgage in principle offer showing he can afford yours. (See Chapters 1 and 4.)

It's a **great moment** when **you get** an offer **for your** property

49

You get an offer for the asking price

Great, but is the buyer serious? Many deals collapse because the buyer can't find a buyer for his own property or is caught up in a long chain which collapses at the wrong moment. Before you accept, check details of your buyer's situation either with your agent or with the buyer himself.

You get several offers at the asking price

Flattering maybe, but this situation needs careful handling. You're likely to be selling in a property boom where there's a shortage of property for sale and buyers are fighting over anything which comes onto the market in an atmosphere of subdued hysteria. Your agent may suggest asking for 'best and final offers', requiring all buyers to lay their cards on the table and name their offer.

Remember that the highest offer isn't necessarily the best. Go for the buyer in the strongest position to go through with the deal, who has his own property under offer and funding provisionally in place, even if the offer is slightly lower. The fewer people involved in any chain the better, which is why first time buyers and those with nothing to sell are valuable commodities. The downside to first time buyers is that they often need to borrow a large proportion of the property's value, which usually means mortgage lenders want to be more thorough about checking out creditworthiness and carrying out valuations. Remember also that it's up to you to choose your buyer (if you have that luxury). Many homeowners decide to deal with a certain buyer because they like them or because a certain buyer is enthusiastic about the property.

The highest offer

isn't necessarily

the best

PLAYING BY THE RULES

Gone are the days when estate agents could describe a damp cupboard as 'a bijou residence with lots of potential' and get away with it. Under the Property Misdescriptions Act, introduced in 1993, agents can be prosecuted and face an unlimited fine for disseminating inaccurate or misleading information about properties. In one case which hit the headlines recently, an agent was prosecuted for doctoring a photograph of a property to remove a tower block next door. In 2000, there were 20 prosecutions under the Act, with offenders incurring fines totalling £73,500. At the time of writing at least eight local trading standards departments were actively pursuing further offenders in their areas. A public register of prohibition orders is kept by the Office of Fair Trading at 3rd Floor, Craven House, 40 Uxbridge Road, Ealing, London W5 2BS.

Agents' activities are also regulated by the Estate Agents Act 1979, updated in 1991. Under this Act, agents must:

- declare conflicts of interest (for example, your agent just knows of a developer who would be very interested in your property, at the right price naturally)

- pass on all offers to you as seller

- tell you as seller if your buyer is taking out a mortgage through the firm's financial services arm.

The OFT has also warned agents that they risk being banned for other 'undesirable practices' such as:

- telling you that you have to sign an agreement with the agency as seller when this isn't a legal requirement.

- putting up 'for sale' boards outside properties which they haven't been instructed to sell. This is a growing problem particularly in London, where several firms have been caught out putting up boards outside

51

> houses divided into flats, obviously hoping that each occupant would think one of his neighbours was selling.

● telling buyers that they won't get onto a 'preferential list' of properties for sale until they take out a mortgage or sell their own home through the agency.

More information from the OFT's website **www.oft.gov.uk** or through the public enquiry line on 08457 224499.

GOING IT ALONE

You don't have to market your property through an estate agent. If you fancy saving yourself agents' commission of around 2 per cent of the sale price of your home, you can sell privately.

But if you're selling your home yourself, be prepared to put in some hard work. You are the one who will have to show people round, maybe two or three times. You will have to keep your marketing information up to date, take all the phone calls, and liaise initially with the buyer's solicitor.

And you will have to organize the advertising. Here you have several options:

● *Newspapers and magazines*. National broadsheets have regular property pages. It's not cheap to place an advertisement but you're paying for it to be seen by more people. For example, the *Times* has property sections on Wednesday and Saturday, the *Telegraph* and the *Independent* on Saturday. The *Sunday Times* and the *Sunday Telegraph* both have well read property sections. In London and the south east the *Evening Standard*'s Homes and Property section comes out on Wednesday. Alternatively, you can use local newspapers or advertise free in *Loot* (**www.loot.com**).

- *On-line*. Several sites have sprung up to provide direct contact between sellers and buyers, hoping to attract sellers to advertise their properties on the site attracted by the prospect of not having to pay agents' commission. Such sites have seen some heavy casualties but one which was still going at the time of going to print was **www.houseweb.co.uk**, which charges sellers £47 to advertise their property on the site with particulars and photographs. You can give details of facilities such as schools and shops nearby and you get a private email box for responses.

3

THE BUYING AND SELLING PROCESS

BY THE END OF THIS CHAPTER YOU WILL

....

- Know when to take excuses for delays with a couple of barrels of salt

....

- Vow to become the world's most efficient filer

....

- Find out more about the property you already own than you ever thought there was to know

....

How the system works now – England and Wales

You've found a property you want to buy. The following outline of what happens when, is relevant to buyers in England and Wales. Information on Scotland follows later in this chapter.

Stage 1: The seller accepts the buyer's offer on his property

The estate agent will write a formal letter confirming the address of the property, the agreed price and the names, addresses and contact numbers of the conveyancing solicitors for both sides. Whether you're buying or selling, you should have found a solicitor or licensed conveyancer to do the legal work by the time you're ready to accept/make an offer.

ACTION POINT ➡

VALUATIONS

Solicitors' fees have risen sharply recently. According to the latest annual Cost of Moving survey from the Woolwich Bank, legal fees for a £50,000 property have risen by an average of 8 per cent year on year and the cost of legal fees on a £200,000 property have risen by 6 per cent. But it's worth it if you can find someone who can do a good job. Residential conveyancing (the legal term for transferring ownership of land or property from one person to another) is widely seen in the legal profession as a bit of a Cinderella task, far removed from courtroom dramas or all-night drafting of multimillion pound deals for corporate clients. Procedures for collecting information have become more standardized and even if you think you're instructing a partner or senior conveyancing solicitor, much of the work will probably be done by juniors or even secretaries. In itself, conveyancing isn't (whisper it softly) difficult but it requires diligence, persistence and a well-organized mind.

Conveyancing isn't difficult

The best advertisement for a solicitor is a word of mouth recommendation from someone who has recently used the same firm for conveyancing. Like most people, solicitors specialize and someone who's a whizz with wills may be, to put it politely, out of practice at conveyancing. Alternatively, go to the Law Society at **www.lawsoc.org.uk** which has a comprehensive database of conveyancing solicitors across the country.

Solicitors' fees vary depending on the value of the property, the complexity of the work (leaseholds, for example, require more work than freeholds) and where you're living/moving to. According to the Woolwich, if you're selling you'll pay on average £374 for a £25,000 property, up to £1858 for a property valued at £1 million pounds. Buying is slightly more expensive, at between £392 and £2003. See Table 3.1 for average costs of buying and selling over different price ranges. But you'll pay a lot more in London and a lot less in the north of England.

If you're buying and selling at the same time, it makes sense to use the same solicitor for both properties.

TABLE 3.1: Selling and buying costs in England and Wales

House price	Selling cost	£	Buying cost	£
£25,000	Solicitor	374	Solicitor	392
	Estate agent	785	Land Registry	40
			Searches	126
			Stamp duty	0
£50,000	Solicitor	388	Solicitor	408
	Estate agent	973	Land Registry	70
			Searches	126
			Stamp duty	0
£80,000	Solicitor	428	Solicitor	449
	Estate agent	1359	Land registry	100
House price	Selling cost	£	Buying cost	£
			Searches	126
			Stamp duty	800

TABLE 3.1: continued *Selling & Buying Costs in England or Wales*

£100,000	Solicitor	459	Solicitor	483
	Estate agent	1660	Land Registry	100
			Searches	126
			Stamp duty	1000
£200,000	Solicitor	596	Solicitor	635
	Estate agent	3910	Land Registry	200
			Searches	126
			Stamp duty	2000
£300,000	Solicitor	732	Solicitor	797
	Estate agent	4688	Land Registry	300
			Searches	126
			Stamp duty	9000
£500,000	Solicitor	1005	Solicitor	1074
			Land Registry	300
			Searches	126
			Stamp duty	15,000
£750,000	Solicitor	1352	Solicitor	1464
	Estate agent	11,314	Land Registry	500
			Searches	126
			Stamp duty	30,000
£1,000,000	Solicitor	1858	Solicitor	2003
	Estate agent	14,988	Land Registry	£500
			Searches	126
			Stamp duty	40,000

Source: Woolwich Bank/University of Greenwich

Stage 2: Solicitors start gathering in the necessary documents

If you're *selling*, your solicitor will:

- *obtain the title deeds to the property*. Unless you own your home outright (in which case the deeds may be with the solicitor who did the conveyancing when you moved to the property you're now selling), these will probably be stored with your mortgage lender. The deeds include Land Registry records showing details of ownership, mortgages, leases, restrictive covenants and boundaries. There will also be a copy of the lease if the property is leasehold, along with details of guarantees for works, planning and building consents and other information on running and maintenance. The most important part of the title deeds as far as your solicitor is concerned is the Land Registry record showing that you own the property that you say you do.

- *ask you to fill in questionnaires about your property*. There are two main forms. The first asks for general information including details of work done to the property, whether there have been disputes with neighbours, who owns and maintains boundary fences and whether the property is a listed building or in a conservation area. The second form has a long list of fixtures and fittings for every room in the house plus the garden with boxes to tick to say whether it's included or excluded in the sale or not relevant. If you live in a leasehold flat, or more rarely a leasehold house, there's a third form to complete, which includes details of who owns the freehold, amounts paid over the past three years in maintenance and service charges and confirmation that insurance premiums are up to date.

- *contact your mortgage lender* to check how much you still owe on loans secured against your home, which will need to be paid back out of the sale proceeds.

- *negotiate a completion date*, when everyone will actually pay over all remaining funds owing, settle up and move house (see Chapter 6). Unfortunately, the completion date, like everything else at this stage in the game, isn't binding and slippages of days, or even weeks, are common.

- *draw up a draft contract to send to the buyer's solicitor.*

Answering the seller's questionnaires to the satisfaction of the buyer's solicitor means collecting and supplying large amounts of back up paperwork. With the new compulsory seller's pack (see Chapter 2), you'll have to do this paperchasing before you put your property on the market. Under the existing system, the starting pistol is fired when you get a buyer. But there's nothing to stop you getting together the following vital papers before you find a buyer – you'll save precious time later:

- *Details of any recent works carried out on the property.* Include specifications (for major works), invoices with breakdowns of work carried out and receipts for payments. Works like damp proofing, dry rot or infestation will normally carry a guarantee which you should produce. Never mind that such guarantees are often not worth the paper they are written on because the company has gone out of business – the object of the exercise is to reassure the buyer's solicitor.

- *Planning permission and building consent documentation* to confirm that any loft extensions, basement conversions or kitchen extensions are above board and not built without the knowledge of the local planning department (see Chapter 6). Modest extensions don't necessarily need planning permission and your local authority should be able to confirm this with a certificate of lawful development.

- *In leasehold flats, the last three years' service charge accounts*, invoices/specifications/receipts for major works and evidence that the buildings insurance organized by the freeholder is up to date. If you own the freehold of your block collectively with your neighbours through a limited company, you will need the memorandum and articles of the company and the certificate showing you own a share of the freehold. If you have a separate freeholder who is inefficient/incompetent/negligent or all three, as many unfortunate leaseholders have (see Inside Track, page 62), this could be a major sticking point. It's not uncommon for leaseholders in a block to receive no accounts at all, accounts that make no sense, non-existent or misleading information about sinking fund money supposedly held in trust or demands out of the blue for thousands of pounds to pay for often unnecessary major works. Start contacting your landlord in good time if you think getting coherent information out of him will be tricky. Any sign that the landlord is difficult will cause problems with the buyer's solicitor.

If you're *buying*, your solicitor will:

- apply to the local authority of the property you are buying for a local search. The cost of this depends on the local authority and fees range from around £90 to £130. Some local authorities take several weeks (although the target turnaround time is 10 days) to produce a search. But the search will give you important information about the property. It will reveal, for example, if there are any proposals for the property under the authority's local development plan, which designates areas as commercial, residential or conservation areas and outlines strategic retail and business centres. You will also discover whether the road on which the property stands is maintained at public expense, and whether the property itself has had planning permission or consents refused or granted. If your seller has breached planning controls, by using a residential building as a business or building illegally, the search will reveal it. But there are plenty of things the search won't reveal. You could move into your new home to find there are advanced plans for a waste disposal plant or that your neighbour is making money by selling off part of his back garden to developers for a block of flats and the search will leave you none the wiser. You won't be told if the land on which your property stands is contaminated unless the council keeps a detailed register, which it's not obliged to.

- report to you details of what the seller has said in response to the standard questionnaires and explain any additional queries he has

One of the things ordinary mortals

swiftly learn is that neither side's solicitors ever read any document

raised with the seller's solicitor. If you're selling your own property, you will also be on the receiving end of 'additional queries', most of which you know you have answered in minute detail already. One of the things ordinary mortals caught up in the housebuying process swiftly learn is that neither side's solicitors ever read any document until the same information has been presented to them several times in different formats and wordings. If you're really unlucky, and especially if you know anything about property, you may discover that you know more than your solicitor and find yourself explaining the difference between a freehold and a leasehold. If you start getting that creepy feeling that the solicitor/client relationship is being reversed, consider changing solicitors.

WEB WATCH

➡ If you want to supplement the information on your search (which in any case you probably won't see unless you specifically ask your solicitor), the following sites are useful (see Chapter 1 for reviews of individual sites): **www.upmystreet.com**; **www.ukonline.gov.uk**; **www.environment-agency.gov.uk**; **www.lganet.gov.uk** (for local authority website list).

INSIDE TRACK

LEASEHOLD VERSUS FREEHOLD

Most houses are owned freehold, which means you own the building and the land it stands on, up to the boundaries of your garden, outright. As long as you keep within the law, you can do what you like with it.

But an estimated two million people live in leasehold properties, where the freehold of the building is owned by a third party. Almost all flats are leasehold, with flatowners responsible individually for their flats. The freeholder is responsible for maintaining, repairing and insuring the building and common parts like stairs and hallways, although leaseholders pick up the bills. More rarely, there are leasehold houses, where the ground the houses stand on is owned by a third party. Either way, being a leaseholder means you have little control over your building. Flatowners who have paid tens or even hundreds of thousands of pounds for their homes are incensed to find that they are technically no more than tenants, with a lease which gives them the right to live in their property for a specific amount of time, commonly 99 years, before the property reverts to the freeholder. The less time the lease has to run, the less it is worth, particularly once the remaining time on the clock is less than 75 years, which is when mortgage lenders start to get twitchy about lending on a depreciating asset.

The leasehold system evolved as a method by which landowners could get their land developed (making lots of money in the process) without selling it outright. Many large cities, including London, grew up this way as builders took leases on development land and in turn leased out the newly built properties. This may have worked well when most people rented their properties on short leases. But now leasehold is becoming increasingly anachronistic, as campaigners for reform have been arguing for the past 30 years.

Successive governments have tinkered at the edges of leasehold law since 1967. The most potentially significant reform, in 1993, was to give flatowners the right to club together to buy their freehold from the landlord, even if the landlord didn't want to sell. Flatowners also won the right to extend their leases by up to 90 years on top of the unexpired term. But, predictably, these rights were so hedged around with complex requirements that few leaseholders took advantage of them. Real pressure for reform erupted in the

63

mid-1990s when a series of media campaigns exposed a widespread catalogue of abuses by unscrupulous landlords. These ranged from demanding huge sums of money for often unnecessary repairs to physical intimidation and threats to repossess the homes of flatowners who refused to pay up. The Conservative Party, traditionally the friend of landlords, found itself in the uncomfortable position of having to pass extensive new laws tightening leaseholders' rights. It was made a criminal offence for landlords not to offer leaseholders first refusal if the freehold was for sale. Leaseholders in dispute with their landlords over management and service charges would in future have their cases heard by a leasehold valuation tribunal (LVT), which would be quicker and cheaper than the county court. The Housing Act 1996 also abolished the right of landlords to forfeit leases of homeowners refusing to pay high service charges unless the charges were deemed 'reasonable' by an LVT. *Leasehold Valuation Tribunal*

Labour came to power in 1997 and pledged to end what it called the 'feudal system' of leasehold. Several consultation papers later, the Commonhold and Leasehold Reform bill finally started its journey through parliament at the beginning of 2001, only to be temporarily stopped in its tracks by the calling of a general election. It was reintroduced in June 2001. It will give leaseholders the right for the first time to club together and set up a management company to take over the management of their building from the landlord or his agent without having to prove negligence or other fault to an LVT as they do currently. (It remains to be seen how practical this will be – the landlord will

The Housing Act 1996 **abolished the right** of landlords to **forfeit leases** of homeowners **refusing** to pay high service charges still be in place as freeholder.) The bill will also introduce commonhold, a new form of tenure which allows flatowners to own their homes outright and collectively become members of a commonhold association responsible for the common parts.

So if the property you want is leasehold, what should you look for?

- Avoid properties with less than 75 years to run unless you know that you can extend the lease without too much expense or hassle. Mortgage lenders are reluctant to lend on anything with less than 50 years to run after the end of a 25-year mortgage term. Leaseholders have the right to extend their leases by up to 90 years, but under current rules you have to have lived in the property for the past three years or three years in the last 10. This creates difficulties if you've been renting out the property long term. The exception to the 'avoid short lease rule' is in central London where shorter leases are common and easily tradeable.

- When you view the property, check the common parts. Are they well maintained? Or do they look as if no one cares? Worn carpets, scruffy paintwork and peeling exterior paint are never a good sign. Suspect a negligent or absentee landlord/leaseholders unwilling to take action/a huge bill for major works looming.

- Make sure your solicitor checks the lease before you buy. The lease sets out your rights and responsibilities in the property. It's a vital defence against a landlord flouting his responsibilities but it's also a weapon for the landlord if you're unwittingly breaking the rules.

- If your solicitor has difficulty getting information about accounts/service charges and so on from the seller, it could point to a landlord who is negligent or just plain inefficient.

- Don't be afraid to ask the neighbours about the landlord's record. And if your solicitor is local and keeps his ear to the ground, he'll be aware of any notorious landlords who have hit the headlines and need to be avoided like the plague.

- Buying a share of the freehold rather than a leasehold property should give you more say in the running of your property. Look for properties advertised as having share of freehold (SoF). Under this arrangement, the leaseholders have clubbed together and bought the freehold through a company set up for the purpose. Each flat holds one share, which is transferred to the new owner when the flat is sold. The freehold company (i.e. you and your neighbours) make all the decisions on running the property and are responsible for insuring it and maintaining its structure. But you are also all still leaseholders in that your lease sets out your rights and obligations. In one of the bizarre anomalies of a bizarre system, you are effectively leasing your properties to yourselves in your position as freeholders.

WEB WATCH

➡ A lifeline for hundreds of thousands of desperate leaseholders is Lease, the government-funded leasehold advisory service. Staffed by a small, dedicated team of leasehold experts, Lease provides free advice to both leaseholders and freeholders and has been an important player in the campaign for leasehold reform. Its website at **www.lease-advice.org** contains a host of useful information including downloadable publications on extending your lease, enfranchisement (i.e. buying your freehold), using a leasehold valuation tribunal and appointing a managing agent. Another site worth checking out, especially if you're the campaigning type, is that of the Coalition for the Abolition of Residential Leasehold (CARL) formed by leaseholders campaigning for reform. Its site at **www.carl.org.uk** has an application form to join the organization, lists of the worst landlord abuses and updates on the progress of leasehold reform.

Stage 3: The buyer organizes surveys and valuations

If you're buying, you need to get valuations and/or surveys organized as soon as possible after you make the offer, while the solicitors for both sides are gathering the papers in. At the risk of teaching experienced property buyers to suck eggs, a valuation is not the same as a survey, although they both value the property as part of the process:

- *Valuation.* Although you pay for it, the valuation is for the benefit of the mortgage lender to check that the property (a) exists and (b) is worth the amount you have asked to borrow. The valuation is fairly cursory (the surveyor won't crawl into loft spaces or burrow into cupboards) and the resulting report is full of blindingly obvious observations ('the property is situated in a residential area close to shops and transport links', 'there is a tree situated in the front garden about 15 feet from the house' etc.) which you could have made yourself. Unfortunately, the majority of borrowers choose (wrongly) to rely on the findings of the valuation (see Inside Track). Until recently, many lenders refused even to let borrowers have sight of the report. Borrowers who subsequently find structural defects after relying on a valuation have little comeback, although court cases have established that the valuer has a duty of care to the borrower as well as the lender. (See Chapter 4 for more on the cost of valuations.)

- *Survey.* This is separate from the valuation and because, unlike the valuation, it is optional, only 20 per cent of buyers opt to pay the extra £500–£800 to have their property properly checked over. Given that you're going to be spending tens or hundreds of thousands of pounds on what you hope will be your dream home, scrimping on a proper survey is, quite simply, a false economy. Surveyors aren't infallible and they've been know to miss things (one of the country's largest surveying firms was taken apart on television for missing obvious defects when filmed with a hidden camera) but they're more likely to spot potentially expensive structural problems than you are. A good local surveyor will also know the area and its history – for example if there's a problem with subsidence as there is in many parts of London and the south east, he may be more relaxed about the odd crack than someone who isn't local. There are two types of survey:

1 *A homebuyer's/flatbuyer's report*. In scope, this is a half-way house between a valuation and a full structural survey. You should expect a fairly thorough inspection of every room, including cellar and loft if accessible, as well as condition of external features like paintwork, roofs, downpipes, drains and guttering.

2 *A full structural survey*. The Full Monty. This should take several hours and include detailed reports on everything mentioned earlier, plus evidence that the surveyor has definitely crawled into the roof space, down into the cellar, peered inside every kitchen cupboard and worked out what heats what, how old items such as the boiler and central heating system are, whether the diagonal crack across from the roof to the top of the window lintel is subsidence (quite possibly, as this is a classic subsidence-type crack) and why the door in the third bedroom sticks.

DID YOU KNOW?

You can save a lot of time and money if you get your valuation and survey done at the same time by the same person. Mortgage lenders normally insist that valuations are done by someone on their surveyors' panel. When your offer is accepted, ask your mortgage lender for names of local surveyors who are on their panel, then contact the firms and get a price from them for doing valuation and survey at the same time. It's good for both sides – they get two lots of business, you get the necessary reports more quickly and the surveyor only has to get access to the property once instead of twice (an important consideration when people are at work during the day). You should be able to get a quote for a lower price carrying out the two together than separately. The Royal Institution of Chartered Surveyors (**www.rics.org.uk**) also has lists of surveyors in your area.

INSIDE TRACK

VALUATIONS

The future and usefulness of the valuation have become a hot issue for mortgage lenders. During the recession of the early 1990s, they found themselves on the receiving end of multimillion pound losses, as borrowers defaulted on their loans in the face of rising interest rates while the value of the properties on which the loans had been secured (based on optimistic 1980s' boom valuations) crashed. It emerged that many valuers had merely carried out 'drive-bys', driving past properties to make sure they were there (and not part of an elaborate mortgage fraud), but not bothering to go inside, so confident were they that prices would go on rising. Lenders and surveyors spent the 1990s locked in acrimonious legal battles. The idea (bizarre in retrospect) that a property had an intrinsic value and could always be sold on at a high enough price to repay outstanding debts was blown apart as millions of borrowers discovered their homes were worth less than the loan secured on them and the term 'negative equity' became part of the horror language of the recession. This bitter lesson learnt, lenders have now developed sophisticated credit-scoring systems for borrowers, arguing that a borrower's ability to pay is as important, or more so, than the supposed value of the property. Some lenders have taken this to its logical conclusion and dispensed with valuations altogether.

Lenders have also come under heavy pressure from government ministers trying to overhaul the creaking housebuying systems with sellers' packs (see later and also Chapter 2). One of the most controversial proposals was that the seller should arrange and pay for a homebuyer's report, which would be included in the seller's pack and which could be relied on by the buyer, and by extension, the buyer's lender. The idea was that this would cut down the time spent trying to get access to properties, value them and write a report, contributing to the overall objective of cutting down the time between offer and exchange of contracts. Lenders initially threatened to derail proposals by insisting on a separate valuation but the Council of Mortgage Lenders (**www.cml.org.uk**) now concedes that this may not be necessary as long as its members have the right to insist on valuations on unusual properties.

Stage 4: The chickens come home to roost

If you're *buying*:

- The surveyor reports to the lender and to you, as buyer, drawing your attention to potential problems with the property. This is mega stress time for both buyers and sellers and is often where a sale comes unravelled.

There are three possible scenarios:

1   The surveyor can't find anything seriously wrong with the property and what's more believes it's correctly priced in the current market. Get out the champagne and wait for your mortgage offer which should be forthcoming in the next few days.

2   There's nothing drastically wrong with the property but the surveyor decrees that it is overpriced. Such downvaluing has been quite common over the past couple of years, particularly in London and the south east, as estate agents and buyers got a bit carried away and surveyors remained ultra cautious in a boom market. A downvaluation is bad news if you need a mortgage because the lender will only lend a proportion of the value put on the property by its surveyor. So if you wanted an 80 per cent mortgage on a £100,000 property and the lender's surveyor values it at £90,000, you would

A downvaluation **is bad news**

if you need a mortgage because

the lender **will only lend** a proportion of

the value put on the property

by its surveyor

only be able to borrow 80 per cent of £90,000. Get out the champagne and drown your sorrows. Then either (a) check all your savings accounts to see if you can dredge up extra money to bridge the gap or (b) see if the seller will reduce the price.

3   The property has what look like potentially problematic structural defects. Get out the gin and don't bother with the tonic. When you've recovered, read between the lines of the report. After the horrible experience of the 1990s, surveyors are desperate to cover themselves, which they do by hedging their bets, outlining a worst case scenario and suggesting that you call in a whole army of other people (structural engineers, drains experts, woodworm and dry rot experts) to produce reports confirming or denying the surveyor's diagnosis. It may not be as bad as it sounds. It's stressful, time consuming and expensive to call in more experts and wait for more reports but at least it gives you either peace of mind or a big bargaining chip to knock down the price. And if the defect is really serious, you'll find out before you make a massively expensive mistake. Mortgage lenders will insist you arrange for all the reports called for by the surveyor. If you still want to go ahead after discovering defects that are expensive to put right, the lender may order a retention of part of the loan until necessary works are done.

Stage 5: Coming up the home straight

Assuming the deal hasn't fallen apart at stage 4, your prospects for actually selling/buying are looking good.

If you're *selling*, your solicitor will:

- *send out the final version of the contract* agreed with the buyer's solicitor for you to sign (or sign it on your behalf if that's what you've agreed). For such a significant transaction, the standard contract is a bit of a disappointment – no seals or flowery language, just a couple of sheets of paper with the names and addresses of the buyer and seller, details of the property, completion date and deposit payable by the buyer. It always used to be standard to ask for a 10 per cent deposit at exchange of contracts when the deal becomes binding. But rising prices have made this more of a struggle. On a £200,000 property – quite a modest sum in many parts of the country these days – a 10 per cent deposit would mean being able to find £20,000 in cash at what is already an expensive time. It's common to negotiate a more nominal sum, although if you're selling, don't let the buyer get away with not paying anything. The deposit is your protection in case, for some reason, the sale doesn't go through after exchange (a very rare occurrence).

If you're *buying*, your solicitor will:

- *get your mortgage offer confirmed*. You may have already had confirmation if your case is straightforward. If there's been a bit of to-ing and fro-ing (downvaluing or potential structural problems for example), you'll get the final confirmation of your offer at this stage.
- *send the agreed amount of deposit to the seller's solicitor*.
- *send you the final version of the contract agreed with the seller's solicitor to sign* (or sign it himself if that's what's agreed).

Contracts are then exchanged (normally over the telephone) and the deal is binding on both sides. Any attempt by either side to wriggle out now will mean expensive legal action. You can afford to relax (as long as you know where all the money's coming from to pay the balance on the agreed completion date).

Stage 6: You complete the sale

In the days of post, telexes and long clearing times for bank drafts, solicitors used to want a leisurely four weeks between exchange and completion. Now it can be done in a week or less, which is fine as long as you are organized and have booked the removal van/told the gas/electricity/telephone/cable companies and started the laborious process of packing and throwing away tons of old rubbish you don't want to take with you (see Chapter 6).

If you're *buying,* you must:

- *make sure your solicitor has the necessary money to pay over to the seller on completion day.* This means that any funds you are putting down yourself, rather than borrowing on a mortgage, need to be sent and cleared. Most banks can transfer funds electronically by the next day, for a fee.

- *check how much the final completion statement is and have the funds ready to cover it.* The completion statement includes the solicitor's conveyancing fee, stamp duty and Land Registry fees.

If you're *selling*:

- your completion statement will also include the estate agent's commission, which the solicitor will pay over to the estate agent.

DID YOU KNOW?

Stamp duty is charged on all purchases of land and property over £60,000 (with rare exceptions, such as when two properties are swapped (see Chapter 8)). On purchases between £60,001 and £250,000, the rate of duty is 1 per cent, on purchases between £250,001 and £500,000 3 per cent and properties over £500,000 4 per cent. No government has yet seized the initiative to abolish stamp duty, although it is looking increasingly anachronistic amid moves to electronic conveyancing (see later). Currently, stamp duty can only be collected on paper transactions where there is something physical to stamp, so, as electronic conveyancing and signatures become a legal and technical reality, stamp duty rules are having to be amended to accommodate the changes. But even this is unlikely to encourage removal of a tax which successive chancellors fondly (and wrongly) believe they can use to direct the housing market.

At the height of the recession stamp duty, then at 1 per cent on all transactions above £60,000, was temporarily abolished to encourage buyers back into the market. More recently Chancellor Gordon Brown jacked up rates on more expensive properties in successive budgets between 1997 and 2001 in the hope of damping down a booming market. Such moves did little more than encourage a temporary blip – tax is not a major consideration if you're buying a million-pound property.

Stamp duty is charged on all purchases of land and property over £60,000

How the future could look – England and Wales

In five years' time, the idea of solicitors, surveyors, lenders and estate agents shuffling pieces of paper backwards and forwards for weeks before buyer and seller physically sign a contract could well look as quaint as adding machines, typing pools or tape spools. Thanks to a combination of long overdue legislative changes and the onward march of email and the internet, the whole housebuying process will take place online, with everyone corresponding electronically and calling up necessary legal documents from vast central databases.

The future should look roughly like this.

Stage 1: The seller decides to put his property on the market

Before he can do so, he must put together a seller's pack containing title deeds, answers to standard questions about the property, a home condition report, a local authority search, details of works carried out and other documents such as leases if relevant. The pack will be prepared either by the estate agent chosen by the seller to market the property, or by his solicitor, by calling up the following documents on screen and either printing them out or packaging them electronically:

1 copies of entries in the Land Register showing ownership, boundaries and mortgages

2 local authority search

3 home condition report arranged by the seller and emailed to the compiler of the seller's pack by the surveyor.

There's a huge amount of work going on behind the scenes at the National Land Information Service (NLIS) **www.nlis.org.uk**, the government agency charged with creating a one-stop property search service, packaging Land Registry entries, local authority searches and other vital documents into one online information file about an individual property. Land Registry (**www.landreg.gov.uk**) information is already available online to solicitors (with plans to give members of the public access), so the real battle is to force local authorities into the twenty-first century and persuade them to computerize their search records.

Stage 2: The property goes on the market

Interested buyers are given a copy of the seller's pack when they make an appointment to view. Instead of having to rely on information from the seller or the evidence of their own eyes, they know at this early stage of any structural or planning problems and can confirm ownership through Land Registry records.

Stage 3: The buyer decides to go for it and make an offer

He will be armed with a mortgage offer in principle, having surfed the net for the best deals before completing an online mortgage application (see Chapter 4).

Stage 4: Solicitors communicate

The buyer's solicitor has the bulk of the necessary information immediately the offer is made (instead of having to start collecting it with weeks of delay). As long as the property is fairly standard, the mortgage lender will not demand a separate valuation but will rely on the homebuyer's report in the seller's pack. (The buyer has the option to have his own survey report, which will lengthen the time between offer and exchange when neither side is committed to the deal.) Solicitors will communicate with each other and with others, like lenders and estate agents, via email.

Stage 5: The two sides sign and exchange contracts electronically

Under current laws, contracts have to be on paper and signed, while transfer documents and mortgage offers are deeds which also have to be on paper, signed and witnessed. But new regulations are being brought in under the Electronic Communications Act 2000 to allow contracts and deeds to be signed electronically and the idea is that everyone should have an individual electronic signature, encrypted for security, as well as a written signature. This will cut out the process of having to have documents posted out for signature.

Stage 6: The deal is done

After both sides sign the deed of transfer electronically and the buyer puts an electronic signature on the final mortgage offer the sale is complete.

Average time between offer and exchange: the Lord Chancellor's Department estimates that e-conveyancing will cut at least eight days off the current typical eight-week gap between offer and exchange with further time saved through sellers' packs.

DID YOU KNOW?

Teramedia, a specialist land and property information company, is working on an online system which will allow you to ascertain how far your transaction has got, who has which documents and what's in the documents, just by logging on and keying in the individual account number allocated to your property. At the beginning of 2001 Teramedia signed the first of four government licences to provide one stop shop online housebuying services. Go to **www.territorium.co.uk** for an update on progress and a free demonstration.

....

The Scottish system

Whenever the subject of reforming the housebuying system in England and Wales crops up, as it does periodically every two or three years, there's a clamour of voices calling for the system in England and Wales to be brought into line with the Scottish system. So what's so great about the Scottish system?

The central difference between the English and the Scottish systems is timing. In Scotland, as soon as a seller accepts an offer, a legally binding contract is created. This means both sides can be certain the deal will go through, there's no scope for gazumping and you don't have the same chains of people all trying to exchange contracts on the same day as you do south of the border.

But what you *do* get in Scotland are a lot of disappointed buyers who have spent money on surveys and valuations on properties they want, only to lose out to a higher bid during the offer process. Bridging loans, which can be expensive and risky (see Chapter 6) are more common in Scotland than in England because buyers often find themselves bound by contract to buy their new home having not sold their current one.

The housebuying process in Scotland works like this.

The **central difference** between

the **English and the Scottish** systems

is timing

Stage 1: You arrange your finances

As in England, this involves checking out the best mortgage deals through lenders, intermediaries and the internet (see Chapter 4). The lender will offer you a mortgage in principle, based on your income and credit rating.

Stage 2: You start househunting, knowing what you can afford

Properties are advertised through estate agents, in newspapers and on the internet as they are in England. But in Scotland, you can also get property details through solicitors' property centres, a solicitor-cum-estate agent arrangement. Solicitors advertise properties for sale, along with basic information for buyers such as a description of the property; fixtures and fittings included in the sale; details of tenancies, obligations and liabilities attached to the property and, most important of all, a price.

Prices will either be fixed, as they usually are in England, or more commonly, offers will be invited over a certain amount, known as the 'upset amount'. You and your solicitor then have to try and second guess the market and find out if you're competing with one or more rival buyers. You won't be told (or at least you shouldn't be) what other offers the seller has received.

Stage 3: You finalize your mortgage offer

This is arranged after the lender has done a valuation and your surveyor has carried out a structural survey. This last is optional but strongly advisable. As in England, the buyer organizes valuations and surveys.

Stage 4: You make your offer

Normally there is a set date, the closing date, by which your offer has to be in. The solicitor makes your formal offer in a letter, called a 'missive', setting out your price and the date you want to complete the sale (the 'date of entry'). The missive will also set out the conditions of the sale. These may cover the following: that there are no problems with rights of way; that roads and mains drainage are maintained by the local authority; that all planning permission and completion certificates for extensions and alterations are available; that the seller owns the property he says he does and that there will be no problems transferring ownership. The seller should produce a 'property enquiry certificate', equivalent to a local search in England and Wales.

Stage 5: Your offer is accepted

This happens usually after several missives have been exchanged between the solicitors acting for the two sides. This is called the 'conclusion of missives' and marks the moment when both sides are bound to the contract and a 'bargain' is made. This is the equivalent of exchanging contracts in England. According to government research, it takes about four weeks on average from making an offer to conclusion of missives, compared with an average of eight weeks between offer and exchange in England and Wales.

Stage 6: The solicitors start the conveyancing process

This involves getting title deeds, checking legal conditions ('burdens and servitudes') affecting the property and checking title. They agree and draft a 'disposition', the document which transfers property ownership to you.

Stage 7: You sign the disposition

You and your lender pay over the money to the seller on the date of settlement, which is usually the same as the date of entry, when you actually take possession of the property.

4

YOUR FINANCES

BY THE END OF THIS CHAPTER YOU WILL

- Know your fixed rates from your discounts and your repayments from your endowments

- Understand where that friendly mortgage adviser at your local bank is coming from

- Resolve to be a reformed character, paying off your debts and saving hard for your deposit.

....
Workings of the mortgage market

Unless you're flush with cash, you'll need to get to grips with the workings of the mortgage market even before you find the property you want. The offer of a mortgage in principle is your passport to being taken seriously by sellers and estate agents (see Chapter 1). But if you're a first time buyer or it's several years since you last needed to read mortgage articles in the personal finance pages instead of throwing them in the bin, you've got some surprises in store.

The mortgage market has changed out of all recognition in the last 20 years. Up until the early 1980s, getting a mortgage meant grovelling to your local bank or building society manager (remember him?) who would insist that you saved with the institution for several years before being granted the privilege of a mortgage. Women had a much harder time of it than men getting a loan. Lenders were unenthusiastic, to put it mildly, about lending on properties built before 1914, which knocks out a substantial chunk of the nation's housing stock. And when you did finally get a mortgage, there was no choice of rates. Building societies, which then dominated the mortgage market, openly operated a cartel which kept all lenders' rates roughly the same. No undercutting, no special deals and no fixed rates. All rates were variable and went up and down in line with the bank base rate.

But this cosy world has been comprehensively blown apart by the dismantling of cartels, easing of restrictions on building societies'

Unless you're flush with cash, you'll need to get to grips with the workings of the mortgage market

A deal you think sounds

the bargain of the century

can turn out to be

an expensive mistake

lending decisions and capital raising powers and the rush of conversions and takeovers which has changed most major building societies from cautious conservative institutions lending on supposedly low risk domestic properties into global financial services companies, desperate to grab a profitable share of the mortgage market. Instead of you having to grovel to them for a loan, they're tempting you with special low fixed rates and discounts, piles of cash upfront, legal fees paid and flexible loans with payment holidays. Some lenders will let you borrow up to four times your income or borrow 100 per cent of the purchase price of your property, largesse not seen since the 1980s mega boom. But they're not doing it out of sheer altruism. The bottom line is that they need to lend you money to make a profit.

Sounds great? Yes and no. The good news is that there's a huge choice of rates and repayment options, particularly if you're a solid, creditworthy citizen with a substantial deposit (of which more later). The bad news is that mortgages have become so complicated that it's almost impossible to compare one product with another and a deal you think sounds the bargain of the century can turn out to be an expensive mistake.

What to look for

There's no such thing as a mere mortgage these days. Variable, fixed, tracker, flexible, capped, discount...a whole new language has developed to describe all the whizzy new products on offer. Not understanding what these terms mean marks you out as an easy target for any bank or building society mortgage 'adviser' (read salesman) and renders internet searches pretty pointless. So here's a rundown of the key types of mortgage you will encounter.

Variable or standard variable rate (SVR)

The most basic type of loan. Still almost certainly the most expensive option for new borrowers, despite a recent twist in the everlasting mortgage war, in which a number of major lenders cut the standard variable rate for new and existing borrowers sharply while reducing the variable rate for those already on discounted loans by much less. With an SVR the rate you pay varies, moving up and down in line with bank base rates. Movements of base rates depend on the state of the economy and most especially on the rate of inflation. Signs of rising inflation are usually choked off by a rise in base rates, which dampens consumer spending. A slowdown in the economy is often countered by a cut in base rates, to stimulate consumer borrowing demand and cut the cost to businesses of borrowing.

In short, with a variable rate loan, you're exposed to all the vagaries of the wider economic climate, which is great when things are going well, the economy is chugging along and interest rates are falling as they were in 2001, but absolutely awful if things go pear shaped, as they did in the recession of the early 1990s when mortgage rates rose to more than 15 per cent. You're also vulnerable to lenders profiting from you by manipulating margins when they're feeling financially squeezed, raising the amount of interest they receive from you as a borrower well above the base rate while slashing the amount they have to pay out to their savers in interest. Don't be seduced by the offer of a 'budget planner' repayment programme on a variable rate loan. All this means is that your repayments will be changed at pre-set intervals during the year rather than moving up or down when base rates do. In a climate of falling rates, you'll be paying over the odds for months until your payments are adjusted. When rates are rising, you'll be shielded from the effects at first before being slammed with a massive rise in payments.

Verdict: Avoid unless you can't get a loan any other way.

Fixed rate

As its name suggests, your rate is fixed for a set term, usually the first two, three or five years, although longer terms have been known. During the fixed rate period your monthly payments stay the same, whatever happens to interest rates. But beware of locking into a fixed rate when base rates generally are falling. What looked like a bargain when you took it out can look very expensive if rates subsequently fall sharply. Coming out of a fixed rate loan early can mean substantial financial penalties. Lenders argue that they have the right to charge penalties for early repayment because they fund fixed rate loans by borrowing from the wholesale markets and borrowers redeeming loans early would leave lenders stuck with funds borrowed at an unprofitable rate. And watch the terms of any fixed rate you sign up for. You could find yourself locked in to staying with the same lender for several more years on an uncompetitive standard variable rate, on pain of a large financial penalty.

Verdict: Can be good if you're on a tight budget or just like to know what your outgoings will be every month.

Capped rate

Your rate can rise but only to a set ceiling, or cap. After this, even if base rates rise, your monthly payment stays the same. If rates fall, so do your mortgage payments. So you get the best of both worlds, safeguarded against unexpected interest rate rises but not locked into high set repayments if base rates fall. The main downside to capped rates is that they tend to be more expensive and rates aren't always competitive.

Verdict: Well worth a look.

Index-tracker

These are a relatively recent innovation, introduced a couple of years ago when lenders were facing fierce criticism for using falls in interest rates to widen the margin between what they charged borrowers and what they paid savers, profiting at customers' expense. An index-tracker rate is variable and it moves up and down in line with base rates. But unlike a standard variable rate, the margin you pay above the base rate is set from the start for a specified period.

Verdict: Not many clear advantages over a fixed or discounted rate.

Discount

You get a set discount off the standard variable rate for the first few years of the loan. During the term of the discount, your monthly bills will fall and rise in line with base rate changes but you'll always be paying at below the standard rate. At the end of the term you revert to a standard rate or switch to a new discount or fixed rate. As with fixed rates, watch that you're not locked in for several extra years on your lender's standard variable rate. A number of lenders have recently muddied the waters by introducing a different, higher standard rate for discounted loans, while offering lower standard variable rates to customers without discounts (see standard variable rates).

Verdict: Good as long as you go for loans with no penalties or lock-in periods.

Flexible mortgage

Another recent innovation but still a niche market. The term flexible mortgage covers a number of different types of loan. With a flexible payment mortgage, you can pay more or less than the usual amount within certain set parameters. When you're feeling flush with cash, you can overpay; when you're feeling poor you can underpay. Overpayments will immediately be credited to your mortgage account, bringing down your total debt. With a current account mortgage, you can combine your current acount and mortgage account into one. Whenever you pay money into your current account, it goes immediately into paying off your mortgage. But it works both ways: whenever you write a cheque or use a debit card, you're effectively borrowing against your mortgage. Some lenders offer a 'sweep facility' where your savings are set against your loan to reduce your outstanding debt. Flexible mortgages have got cheaper as more products appear on the market although they're still more likely to have standard variable rates than fixed rates.

Verdict: Good for the self-employed and those on irregular incomes but require discipline.

Figure 4.1 How to find the right mortgage for you

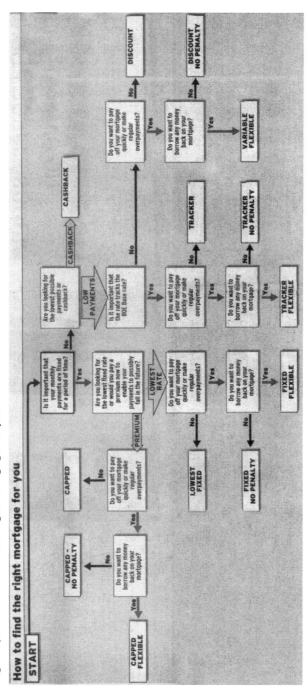

How to find the right mortgage for you

Source: LONDON & COUNTRY MORTGAGES 0800 373300 www.lcplc.co.uk

WEB WATCH

➡ The following lenders are active in the flexible loan market: Woolwich (**www.woolwich.co.uk**), Bank of Scotland (**www.bankofscotland.co.uk**), Intelligent Finance (**www.if.co.uk**),Virgin Direct (**www.virgindirect.com**).

Checklist

Whatever type of loan you go for, ask probing questions about fees, costs, penalties and any compulsory insurances before signing anything. The Department of Trade and Industry's website at **www.dti.gov.uk** has some useful information for prospective mortgage borrowers including checklists of questions to ask. This list should include:

- *arrangement fees*. Special deals (discounts, fixed rates, capped rates) usually cost money. Expect to pay an arrangement fee of between £200 and £500, either on completion of your sale or upfront before the sale goes through. If the fee is payable on completion, you won't have to pay up if your sale falls through, although you will if you have to produce the money upfront. But such is the competition in the mortgage market at the moment that you may get your arrangement fee refunded, especially if you're a first time buyer. Alternatively there are fee-free deals around, although lenders will usually claw the money back in another way, in higher rates for example. It can be tempting to accept a lender's offer to add the fee to the outstanding debt, especially if you're strapped for cash but remember you'll be paying interest on it for the whole of the mortgage term. *Note*: You shouldn't have to pay an arrangement fee for a standard variable rate.

- *valuation fees*. Most lenders will insist on a valuation to confirm the property is worth at least the amount you want to borrow (see Chapter 3). The fee is levied on a sliding scale depending on the value of the property and what you pay depends partly on the deal between lender and surveyor – volume valuations sometimes mean discounts

You shouldn't have to pay an arrangement fee for

a standard variable rate

for lenders which can be passed on to you. Expect to pay around £150 for a £50,000 property and around £250 for a £200,000 property. Some of the best deals (at the time of writing) waived or refunded valuation fees.

- *penalties for early redemption.* These have been a controversial subject in the mortgage industry ever since interest rates started falling as the recession tailed off and it started to make financial sense for borrowers to fix their rates. Lenders borrow money for fixed rates from the wholesale markets then hope to make a profit on the turn between what they've paid for the wholesale funds and the rate at which they sell the funds on to borrowers at fixed or discounted rates. To stop borrowers from cashing in their loans before the end of the fixed or discounted term, leaving lenders with expensively purchased funds they couldn't sell on, lenders started to levy hefty penalties for early redemption. These tactics were later extended so that borrowers found themselves 'locked in' beyond the end of the fixed or discounted period, stuck in a usually uncompetitive standard variable rate for two or three further years on pain of large penalties if they left. The Council of Mortgage Lenders (**www.cml.org.uk**), the lenders' trade body and creator of the industry's code of mortgage lending (see A dog's dinner? later), stopped short of recommending a ban on redemption penalties. The CML's argument was that such a move would restrict consumer choice. If lenders were allowed to levy penalties, they could offer lower rates to borrowers on tight budgets, while offering an alternative of higher rates and no penalties for people who were happy to pay more for the option of being allowed to cash in early if they wanted. But the can of worms had been opened and there's now plenty of choice of loans with no lock-in periods at all or no lock-ins beyond the end of the special deal period.

- *mortgage indemnity guarantee (MIG)*. If you need to borrow a big proportion of the property's value (more than 90 per cent), you will almost certainly have to pay a one-off mortgage indemnity insurance premium. Although you pay the premium, it covers the lender in case your home has to be repossessed and sold at a loss, as happened to hundreds of thousands of homeowners in the recession. And the sting in the tail is that lenders still reserve the right to chase you for any shortfall after the policy has paid out if they believe further down the line that you can afford to pay it back (see Did You Know?). Most lenders have stopped charging MIG for loans of between 75 per cent and 90 per cent of a property's value following widespread criticism of the practice. But MIG premiums can set you back hundreds or even thousands of pounds depending on the lender, the amount you want to borrow and the value of the property.

  If this is 'kindly' added to the outstanding debt, you'll be paying interest on it throughout the mortgage term. Avoid MIGs if possible by saving up a bigger deposit before you buy or looking for MIG-free deals, of which there is a growing choice.

- *compulsory insurance*. A rip-off with a capital R. Taking out buildings and contents insurance with your lender is an expensive option because premiums include substantial commissions to lenders from insurance companies. There's been a lot of talk about outlawing 'tie-ins' as they're known in the industry, but nothing has yet materialized. Don't be tempted to go for a deal which has a low rate conditional on taking out the lender's buildings and contents insurance. What you save on the rate, you'll spend on more expensive insurance. Similarly don't go for a deal with a low rate which is conditional on taking out an endowment policy. Endowments are an expensive, inflexible and widely discredited repayment (see Inside Track on endowments later in this chapter).

CAT marks

You may see references to CAT-marked mortgages in lenders' marketing blurb. CAT stands for charges, access, terms and CAT marks are part of a big government push to bring lenders to heel and force them to make mortgage conditions and charges easier and clearer to understand. Ministers particularly hate redemption penalties which lock borrowers in after the end of fixed rate or discount terms, hidden fees and interest-charging structures which benefit lenders not borrowers. The main features of CAT standard loans are:

- *For variable rates*:

  – no arrangement fees

  – interest calculated daily

  – no redemption charges at any time

  – interest rates no more than 2 per cent above base rate

  – mortgage rates adjusted within one month when base rates fall.

- *For fixed or capped rates*:

  – maximum booking fee of £150

  – maximum redemption charge of 1 per cent of the amount you owe for each remaining year of the fixed period, with no redemption charge after the end of the fixed rate period

  – no redemption penalties if you stay with the same lender when you move house.

All CAT-marked loans must be available to new and existing customers and portable so that you can take them with you when you move house.

Capital repayments to reduce your mortgage debt will be credited to the mortgage account immediately. Brokers cannot charge fees for introducing CAT standard mortgages. CAT marks also apply to loans of £10,000 or less to benefit people remortgaging with small loans.

But beware: CAT-marked loans aren't necessarily the best deal. Lenders have been unenthusiastic, warning that offering CAT-marked loans will reduce their opportunities to subsidize competitive deals with more expensive rates, and complaining that administration and systems costs to calculate interest daily will be costly.

Table 4.1 shows levels of monthly repayment on mortgages of different amounts (down the left-hand column) at different rates of interest (across the top).

TABLE 4.1: What your mortgage will cost

	5%	6%	7%	8%	9%	10%
£30,000	£177.38	£195.57	£214.53	£234.20	£254.52	£275.42
£40,000	£236.51	£260.76	£286.04	£312.26	£339.35	£367.23
£50,000	£295.64	£325.94	£357.54	£390.33	£424.19	£459.03
£60,000	£354.76	£391.13	£429.05	£468.39	£509.03	£550.84
£70,000	£413.89	£456.32	£500.56	£546.46	£593.87	£642.65
£80,000	£473.02	£521.51	£572.07	£624.53	£678.71	£734.45
£90,000	£532.14	£586.70	£643.58	£702.59	£763.55	£826.26
£100,000	£591.27	£651.89	£715.09	£780.66	£848.39	£918.07

Source: Council of Mortgage Lenders

Strapped for cash or complex case?

Financial puritans would say you shouldn't even be thinking about a loan if you're strapped for cash. But low mortgage rates and a steady economy have made buying a more attractive and cheaper proposition for many people than renting and survey after survey shows that a majority of people in the UK aspire to home ownership. So what if you haven't got a deposit to put down or your income is irregular but you're still confident you can afford to keep up mortgage payments?

100 per cent loan

You borrow 100 per cent of the price of the property from your mortgage lender. This may sound great (a bank or building society lends you a big dollop of money and you get the property you want without having to produce any funds upfront yourself) but it's a risky strategy. If house prices fall sharply as they did in the recession of the early 1990s, you could find yourself in negative equity, when your property is worth less than the value of your mortgage, unable to sell unless you can fund the shortfall yourself. This may all seem theoretical and unimportant at a time of rising house prices and general prosperity but as millions of people trapped in negative equity will testify, the economy can turn from boom to bust in a terrifyingly short space of time. And the downturn destroyed many people's jobs and businesses, leaving them unable to pay their mortgage bills, pushing them into spiralling arrears until lenders lost patience and repossessed their homes.

Self-certification loan

You don't have to provide evidence of your income as part of your loan application. Self-certification can be useful if you're self-employed, have irregular income or no documentary evidence of an income stream. But this is a niche market. Only a small number of lenders offer these loans, and you'll pay for the increased risk lenders are taking with higher interest rates, more stringent conditions and more onerous penalties.

Shared ownership

There are a number of schemes aimed at buyers who can't afford to buy a property outright. Conventional shared ownership allows you to buy a share of a property, usually between 25 per cent and 75 per cent and rent the rest from a social landlord, usually a housing association. You can buy further shares as and when you can afford it until you own the whole property. Priority on this scheme is given to existing council tenants, tenants of social landlords and those on housing waiting lists.

A variation on conventional shared ownership is do-it-yourself-shared-ownership (DIYSO). Under this scheme, you choose your own property on the open market, then borrow between 25 per cent and 75 per cent of the value on a mortgage (50 per cent is the average). You pay rent to a social landlord on the remaining portion. DIYSOs are on offer through a limited number of local authorities. There's no longer a national DIYSO scheme – ministers decided the terms were too generous and replaced DIYSO with the Homebuy scheme in 1999. With Homebuy, people in social housing or on waiting lists can buy a property on the open market with an interest-free loan for 25 per cent of the value from a social landlord. The remaining 75 per cent is funded through a normal mortgage and/or savings. When the property is sold, 25 per cent of the value of the property at the time it's sold is paid back to the social landlord. The thinking behind this scheme is to free up social housing for people in real need and give slightly better off people a leg up onto the housing ladder.

DID YOU KNOW?

If you get into difficulties with mortgage payments, don't think you can run away from your debts by handing your keys in and doing a disappearing act. Lenders claim they have up to 12 years to chase you for repayment of any shortfall they are left with if they have to repossess your home and sell it at a loss. Advice agencies like the National Association of Citizens' Advice Bureaux (NACAB **www.nacab.org.uk**) argue that it's a moot legal point whether mortgage lenders have the right to a 12-year time lapse and say the time limit should be six years, in line with other debts. The Council of ▶

> Mortgage Lenders persuaded most of its members to sign up to a protocol pledging that they won't chase borrowers for outstanding debts incurred more than six years previously if no initial contact has been made within that six years. But whether it's six or 12 years, the point is that you can't write off your debt by handing in your keys. If you're in difficulties with mortgage payments, tell your lender and negotiate a payment schedule that you can stick to.

Repayment methods explained

Once you've chosen what sort of loan you want (see What to look for), you then have to choose how to repay it. As a general rule, you should expect to be able to repay any type of loan in any way you want. (If a lender insists on setting up a loan as an endowment in return for a good rate, go elsewhere.) Your basic choices are as follows.

Repayment loan

The simplest sort of loan. Your monthly mortgage payment is a mixture of interest and capital, so you start paying off your loan immediately. At first most of the repayment is interest, with the capital element increasing as a proportion towards the end of the loan. The exact calculations are fairly opaque. All you see is the total mortgage payment going out each month and an annual statement showing how much of your outstanding debt (pitifully little at first) you've paid off over the

Don't think you can run away from your debts by handing your keys in and doing a disappearing act year. The vital thing about a repayment loan is that it's guaranteed to pay off your mortgage at the end of the term, unlike an endowment.

Verdict: The safest and cheapest sort of loan for most people. Don't be misled by salesmen who warn you that repayments are 'less flexible' than endowments, that you will have to start from scratch if you move house and that you'll be paying off your mortgage for the rest of your life. This isn't true: you can start a new repayment loan over a shorter term.

Interest-only loan

Your monthly mortgage repayment includes only interest. Alongside this you set up a separate investment fund, into which you pay regularly to build up enough money to pay off your loan at the end of the mortgage term. Some lenders don't even ask how you're planning to repay your loan – they just set it up on an interest-only basis and trust you to make appropriate arrangements. (If you don't, you'll either have to hope a rich relation dies and leaves you a big inheritance or sell your home to pay off the mortgage, even if you don't want to move.) But the investment isn't guaranteed to pay off your loan. If you move house you can take your investment pot with you and top it up if you need to.

Verdict: Fine if you're happy to take the risk of investing in the stockmarket and take on the commitment of paying into an investment long enough to build up a large lump sum. But make sure you know what you're buying – some policies appear to be designed mostly with an eye to generating maximum commission for salesmen for minimum effort.

Which investment?

There are three common types of mortgage-linked investments.

Endowment

This is a stockmarket investment and life assurance policy combined. The idea is that you build up enough in your investment fund over the mortgage term (usually 25 years) to pay off your mortgage. If you die during the term, the policy pays off the loan for you. Endowments can either be 'with profits' or 'unit linked'. With profits policies are meant to be lower risk, smoothing out peaks and troughs in the stockmarket with annual bonuses, which can't be taken away once they're attached, and a terminal bonus at the end, reflecting the state of the market at the time. With a unit-linked policy, your premiums are invested in units linked to a mixture of equities, fixed interest investments (gilts and bonds) and cash. What you get at the end depends on the state of the market at the time and there are no annual bonuses, which makes unit-linked policies a bit riskier than with profits. But there are big problems with endowments (see Inside Track).

Individual savings account (ISA)

You can put up to £7,000 this tax year (2001-2002) into an ISA, which pays tax-free returns. With a maxi ISA you can invest up to £7,000 in a mixture of cash, shares and insurance. For a mortgage-linked ISA, investing the £7,000 in shares is more likely to produce the best returns, although as the well-worn phrase goes, past performance is not a guide to the future. If you take out a mini ISA (maximum investment £3,000) you can't have a maxi ISA in the same year. ISAs replace tax efficient special savings schemes (TESSAs) and personal equity plans (PEPs).

You can make regular monthly payments or pay in lump sums to build up capital to pay off a loan. You can change your ISA provider every year if your current one isn't performing well. Like pensions or endowments, ISAs aren't guaranteed to pay off your loan. Unlike a pension or endowment you can get at your money at any time without penalty. But if you're saving up to pay off a mortgage, you must avoid such temptations.

Pension

The main reason for linking a pension to a mortgage is that pensions attract generous tax breaks. You get tax relief on contributions at your highest rate of tax and you can take 25 per cent of the resulting fund on retirement as a tax-free lump sum to pay off your mortgage. But take advice before harnessing your pension to your mortgage. Personal pensions can carry expensive upfront and ongoing charges (although the new generation of stakeholder pensions represents better value) which cut the amount of your contribution actually being invested. And pension providers now get less generous tax relief on the money they're investing on your behalf, which means your fund grows at a slower rate. As with other sorts of stockmarket investment, returns aren't guaranteed and if your pension performs poorly you risk having to use part of a smaller than expected pension fund to pay off your loan.

INSIDE TRACK

ENDOWMENT MORTGAGES — ARE THEY A RIP OFF?

Endowment mortgages used to be the most popular way of repaying a loan and millions were sold in the boom years of the late 1980s. But since then, there's been a massive backlash, with widespread criticism of endowments as an expensive and inflexible way to repay a mortgage.

Worse still, it has gradually emerged that unscrupulous insurance salesmen (many employed by big name insurance companies and banks) could have misled homeowners into believing (wrongly) that their endowment was guaranteed to pay back their mortgage. Falling stockmarkets, falling interest rates and lower inflation have combined to slash returns and millions of homeowners have now been told their policies will *not* pay off their mortgages. Insurance companies are now having to pick up the tab for switching borrowers into repayment loans and the whole fiasco has so far cost £25 million.

In the mid-1980s when returns from endowments were high thanks to a booming stockmarket, some bright spark in the insurance industry conceived the idea of the low cost endowment. By making certain (in retrospect very optimistic) assumptions about investment returns, insurance companies could cut the cost of premiums and thus market endowments to a mass audience of eager borrowers. One big selling point of endowments was that proceeds were usually tax free and many borrowers were seduced by promises of big tax-free lump sums remaining after the mortgage was paid off.

A major drawback with many endowments is that they can carry hefty upfront charges and annual management charges. In some cases almost all your investment in the early years goes towards paying salesmen's commission and the insurer's administration charges. If you surrender the policy early, as nearly three-quarters of with profit policy holders do, you're unlikely to get your money back. And because terminal bonuses now make up nearly two-thirds of the final payout on with profits policies, you'll miss out on a huge chunk of cash.

Most independent financial advisers say there are almost no circumstances in which an endowment mortgage is clearly the best option. They are particularly inappropriate for young, single people with no dependants whose circumstances could change dramatically over the next 25 years. A repayment mortgage with separate term assurance (which pays out if you die during the term and doesn't if you don't) is a lot cheaper and simpler.

Where to shop for your mortgage

Once you know roughly what all the jargon means and are confident you can keep your end up in a mortgage interview without looking foolish, start shopping around. Unless you're a hopeless case, with a list of county court judgments as long as your arm and a zero-rated credit score, banks, building societies and mortgage brokers will be falling over themselves to lend you money. But it pays to know where they're coming from.

Banks and building societies

They dominate the high street, they have big advertising and marketing budgets and their mortgage 'advisers' have high sales targets. They make their money by selling you expensive investments, especially endowments. Most of them (with some honourable exceptions, the Bradford & Bingley for example) sell only their own products, so you will be offered that lender's mortgages, pensions, endowments and other investments. Historically, building societies and former building societies like the Halifax and Abbey National have offered better mortgage rates than the big banks like Barclays or Lloyds TSB but it's almost impossible to generalize because the mortgage market is so competitive and strategies change almost overnight. The major players now also have internet arms (see later) with different and often better rates for borrowers prepared to use the net. Be very wary of buying investments

Once you know roughly
what all the jargon means

start shopping around

from the insurance arms of big banks – performance has traditionally been indifferent and charges high.

Verdict: Avoid endowments but worth getting quotes on rates. Check small print carefully for penalties (see Checklist earlier).

Estate agents

Many estate agency chains were bought up in the 1980s by financial services companies who saw this as an ideal way to sell lots of endowment mortgages and related insurance to homebuyers. Many agents who weren't bought up by insurance companies nonetheless became tied agents, committed to selling investments of only one company. The virtual collapse of the endowment market has made this less lucrative but estate agents, particularly at the mass market end of the scale, can still be pushy about trying to arrange your loan for you, even before you've found a property. Confusingly, estate agents can get away with calling themselves 'independent mortgage advisers'. They can quite legitimately be tied to one insurance company for endowments or other regulated investments, while arranging loans with a variety of lenders. Mortgage lending and advice are currently unregulated (although this is set to change; see A dog's dinner?) and they can parade their 'independence' while playing down their links to insurance companies who pay their commission. Remember, it is illegal for estate agents to force you to take out a mortgage with their financial services arm as a condition of viewing properties.

Verdict: Can be useful for no-obligation quotes to give you a feel for what's on the market but you risk being pestered to sign up for a mortgage if you look too keen. Fine if that's what suits you but you can get information on rates and deals more restfully by surfing the net.

Independent financial advisers (IFAs)

They are registered and regulated for investment business by the Financial Services Authority (**www.fsa.gov.uk**). Under FSA rules, IFAs have to offer suitable advice over a whole range of investments from different companies, rather than just those of one company, so you've got more chance of getting something that is (a) suitable, (b) good value for money and (c) a consistently strong performer. Most IFAs are also registered under the lending industry's voluntary mortgage code (see later) to offer independent mortgage advice or information. IFAs either charge fees, usually a percentage of the mortgage loan, or they are paid by the lender for introducing mortgage business. This means (or should mean) that they aren't driven by the need to earn commission and meet sales targets to sell you an endowment.

Verdict: Worth paying for, particularly if you have tricky or unusual requirements or a checkered credit history.

The internet

Almost all lenders have their own sites and many operate internet-only loans with keener rates than those available on the high street. But there are also growing numbers of mortgage broker sites, offering mortgage calculators so that you can work out how much you can afford to borrow and how much the true cost of your loan will be.

Verdict: An excellent way to start your search. It can be totally impersonal, with none of the obligation you may feel confronted by an obviously desperate salesperson. You can also apply for your loan online although, to date, an application is about as far as you can get without having to produce some written paperwork (evidence of income and so on). In the brave new e-world promised by Labour in its first term, you should eventually be able to complete the whole process online with an electronic signature (see Chapter 3).

WEB WATCH

➡ As with everything on the internet at the moment, the online mortgage sector is in a state of flux, with sites emerging and disappearing in a matter of months, often after an initial flurry of high profile advertising. In the time it took to research this book, at least three mortgage broking sites – E-loan, Moneygator and NetMortgage – closed for business. The reality is that most mortgage broking sites survive by advertising and there's only a finite amount of advertising business around. But the Darwinian tussle between rival sites shouldn't concern you overmuch as a consumer. What all the following sites do more or less efficiently is to sift through the mass of rates, conditions and special offers and produce a shortlist of potentially suitable mortgages. Although you have to register to apply online, you shouldn't have to register or pay a fee either to search the site or to use the mortgage calculator which works out how much you can afford and what different loans over different time periods really cost.

➡ www.moneysupermarket.co.uk

Background: Online mortgage broker.

Claim: A choice of 4000 variable, fixed, capped and discounted mortgages as well as more specialist loans for right to buy, buy to let and self build properties (see later chapters) and self-certification loans (see earlier).

How it works: Lists current best buys in every sort of category – fixed, capped and discount loans, with no redemption penalties, penalties only if you cash in the loan before the end of a special deal term, and extended penalties lasting after the end of the deal term. What this overview demonstrates, apart from what's on the market, is that there's no such thing as a free lunch. There are some low rates around but you'll face penalties if you leave that lender even several years after the end of the special deal. Some lenders offer thousands of pounds of cashback money but you'll pay for it with a higher rate.

➡ Rates which don't look that low at first sight will work out cheaper over the longer term. This is why you need a mortgage calculator, now a valuable feature of most broker sites. The most useful sum on the calculator is the one which works out the true cost of your loan over any period you choose (five and seven years are popular because that's the length of time, on average, people stay in one property). The true cost includes arrangement fees and upfront costs and deducts cashbacks or other payouts. You will need to input details of your income and credit history, explain why you want the money (property purchase or remortgage for example) and where you want to look (bank, building society, broker, specialist lender). You don't commit yourself to anything by providing this information.

Pros: Easy-to-use site with obvious links to other pages.

Special feature: Mortgage auction where lenders compete for your business. The site claims £300 million of mortgage applications have been obtained by this route to date. For a £10 fee you submit an application and wait for eager lenders to email you in three working days.

Verdict: Workmanlike and thorough.

➡ www.moneynet.co.uk

Background: Independent online mortgage adviser.

Claim: Independent of all providers. 'We don't operate from a restricted panel of product providers and make no charge for inclusion.' Claims to have mortgages from more than 100 lenders.

How it works: Includes information on residential mortgages, buy to let loans and remortgages (useful if interest rates are falling and you're worried that you're paying too much on your existing loan). It can sort loans either by lowest headline rate (i.e. the rate in big print on advertising material), by largest cashback rate or by total cost of product (see Where to shop for your mortgage) with the lowest first. Mortgage calculators let you work out how much you can borrow, how much it will cost and how much you can afford to repay.

Pros: Easy-to-use, clear site with lots of information including sound advice in the form of frequently asked questions (FAQs) on issues like 100 per cent loans and mortgage indemnity insurance.

Cons: Despite claims to be updated daily, answers to FAQs ignored the existence of individual savings accounts (ISAs) and discussed personal equity plans (PEPs) which haven't been on sale for several years. Constant flashing advertisements for financial services companies were also distracting (although it's a price borrowers have to pay if they don't fancy the alternative – paying for the information).

Special feature: Rate alert service alerts you by email to new interesting rates. Finance directory provides links to wide range of lender and broker sites.

Verdict: Good site once the out-of-date parts have been updated.

➡ www.moneyextra.com

Background: Independent financial adviser.

Claim: Access to 4500 variable, fixed, capped and discounted rates along with more niche products including flexible loans and self-certification loans.

How it works: Produces a list of possible loans when you input value of property, value of loan required and your income. You can refine searches by excluding deals with compulsory insurance or extended redemption penalties for example. A good feature is the quick calculator which allows you to change one or more of the variables to get a different result.

Pros: Useful definitions of jargon (repayment, endowment and so on) pop up when you click on words as you work through the mortgage search.

Cons: The site is a bit texty and messy although it's going through a revamp at time of writing. Flashing advertising is an irritant. And there was no obvious link to an explanation of the mortgage code and whether the site is registered. Even if the information was there, it wasn't prominently enough displayed.

Verdict: Revamp will be welcome but information provided is solid enough.

Also worth a look: **www.fredfinds.com**. The Fred Finds lark, with cartoon character Fred, is about as irritating as Hector the Tax Inspector, i.e. very irritating indeed. But easy to use and there's a clear explanation of how the site is regulated.

A dog's dinner? Mortgage regulation

The more complicated the mortgage market becomes, the more vulnerable borrowers are to taking out an unsuitable loan. Given the amounts usually involved in house purchase, signing up for the wrong mortgage can be a costly mistake. Labour came to power in 1997 pledged to tighten mortgage regulation and consumer protection. Changes are in the pipeline. But, to date, mortgage regulation is a dog's breakfast, to put it politely. Here are the basics:

- Sales of mortgage linked investments like endowments or pensions are regulated by the Financial Services Authority. Anyone selling investments must be registered and qualified and must be able to demonstrate that the policy they've recommended you is suitable. All registered firms and individuals are inspected by regulators and can face fines or expulsion from the industry if they break rules.

- By contrast, information and advice on mortgages is currently regulated only by industry voluntary agreement under a code of mortgage practice sponsored by the Council of Mortgage Lenders. Most lenders and brokers, including estate agents and independent mortgage advisers, are signed up to the code and lenders bound by the code have to agree not to accept business from any broker not signed up. But a minority of fringe players don't want to play by these rules and no one can make them.

The more complicated the mortgage market becomes, the more vulnerable borrowers are to taking out an unsuitable loan

- The mortgage industry has cleaned up its act significantly since the code was introduced in 1997, with compulsory training qualifications, tighter monitoring and mystery shopping expeditions by the Mortgage Code Compliance Board (**www.mortgagecode.org.uk**), which is responsible for the operation of the code. But a recent survey for *Which?* magazine found that of 48 lenders, estate agents and advisers, only one had given 'all round good advice' and compliance with requirements to explain to borrowers their rights under the code was patchy.

- After a decent interval to see how the code and self-regulation were working, ministers bowed to pressure from consumer groups and, more belatedly the Council of Mortgage Lenders, and announced plans for statutory regulation of mortgage lending and advice by the Financial Services Authority (FSA), which already polices sales of endowments, pensions and other investments linked to mortgages. But controversially, the Treasury ignored pleas for a commonsense approach which would have seen mortgage brokers and advisers individually registered and regulated directly with the FSA.

  Instead, mortgage lenders will be responsible for policing standards of advice and information provided by intermediaries with whom they do business, a solution that pleases no one.

- It looks likely that most of the code will be incorporated in some way into mortgage regulation but it's not yet clear how.

- The explosion of mortgage broking sites on the internet has exposed a number of grey areas in mortgage regulation, particularly with regard to which sites have to be regulated by the mortgage code and which can avoid being bound to it by claiming status as an 'introducer'. Technically, sites which offer only information or which merely introduce borrowers to sites registered with the code don't themselves have to be regulated. But there's a thin dividing line in the brave new world of e-mortgages between information and advice.

- Does it matter if you deal with an unregistered intermediary/lender/website? Yes, because you have little or no comeback if you think you've been sold a pup. Firms or sites signed up to the mortgage code have to be members of the relevant ombudsman or arbitration scheme which can investigate complaints and make decisions binding on both sides (see Action Point). Unregistered firms face no such requirement. Check that a firm is registered by calling the Mortgage Code Compliance Board helpline on 01785 218200.

ACTION POINT ➡

HOW TO COMPLAIN

- Complain to the firm that sold you the policy/mortgage and go through its internal complaints procedure.

- If you are unhappy with the firm's decision, approach the relevant complaints body. For mortgage advisers employed directly by lenders, or complaints about lenders generally, contact the Financial Ombudsman Service (020 7964 1000, **www.financial-ombudsman.org.uk**).

- For mortgage lenders which aren't building societies or banks but which are signed up to the mortgage code, contact the Chartered Institute of Arbitrators (020 7421 7444, **www.arbitrators.org**) which operates the mortgage code arbitration scheme.

- If your complaint is about a mortgage broker, contact the Chartered Institute of Arbitrators which may be able to help if the firm is registered under the code.

- Complaints about endowments, pensions and other investments are handled by the Financial Services Authority (020 7676 1000, **www.fsa.gov.uk**) and dealt with by the Financial Ombudsman Service.

What to expect under the code

1   You should be told at the outset whether the firm/site is registered with the code and given a copy of the leaflet *You and Your Mortgage*, which sets out the minimum standards you can expect. If you're surfing the net look for an icon or link which will give you details. *You and Your Mortgage* is also available online at **www.cml.org.uk**.

2   There are three levels of service under the code: (a) information on a single mortgage product (if that's all that's available or you already know what you want); (b) information on different types of mortgage on offer so that you can make an informed choice; (c) advice and recommendation on the most suitable mortgage. With (c) you should expect to be taken through details of your income and circumstances, known in the industry as a factfind.

3   Mortgage brokers should tell you if they are acting as an agent or appointed representative for the lender or if they are independent, acting for you and checking the whole market for the best deal.

4   Brokers should disclose any fees they stand to receive from lenders for introducing your business.

Applying for your loan

Searching for the most suitable mortgage deal is just the first step. There's a long trail of information and paperwork to supply before you get a final mortgage offer.

Applying in person

At this stage you should have narrowed down your choice to a handful of lenders/brokers which appear to be offering potentially suitable mortgage deals. You will be asked to make an appointment with a mortgage adviser, who will ask you details of your income and circumstances. Depending on what you want and what the adviser is qualified to offer, you may have to make a second appointment. This is common practice if you want an interest-only mortgage linked to an investment, because the person with whom you are discussing the mortgage may not be qualified to advise on investments (see A dog's dinner?). At the first appointment you should expect the adviser to explain his or her position under the mortgage code (see earlier). The adviser will then give you information/advice, making it clear which one it is and do a credit check (see box). Credit checks are now the work of a moment as it's all done electronically and the adviser's computers will be searching the relevant databases to check you out while you're talking.

Applying over the internet/by phone

The process is similar – you complete a form detailing your circumstances and income and send it online to the lender or broker offering the most suitable deal for you. Note that online mortgage advice is rare. Don't apply online if you don't feel confident of being able to interpret the information given.

If you pass the checks, you will be offered a mortgage in principle. The final mortgage offer doesn't come until the property you want has been valued and checked out to see it's worth the loan you want.

ARE YOU CREDITWORTHY?

Credit referencing is more sophisticated than it's ever been, as lenders refine their techniques for assessing whether you're good for a loan, and more importantly, that you'll continue to be good for it. You'll score well if you're:

- *married*. Marriage spells commitment, reliability and borrowers who can't chuck it all in and go and live on an island in the Caribbean even if they want to. Co-habiting or divorced couples score less well. ▷

- *a homeowner, particularly if you've got a good mortgage repayment record.* You've demonstrated that you can handle financial commitment. Unfairly, being a good tenant and paying the rent on time doesn't rate as highly.

- *in a steady job.* Lenders love you if you have regular wage slips and a solid staff job, notwithstanding the sorry truth that there's no such thing as a job for life. They're much less keen on the self-employed despite the growing army of self-employed and short-term contract workers. Expect to have to produce mountains of paperwork, accounts and letters of glowing recommendation from accountants if you work for yourself or have a portfolio of contracts.

- *have a deposit.* The bigger your deposit, the greater the commitment it demonstrates in the eyes of the lender.

- *are creditworthy and genuinely exist/live where you claim to.* Online checks will access your details on the electoral roll and look up your credit record. Evidence of financial probity in the form of regular repayments will bump up your score.

- *can handle your other financial commitments.* Lenders apply a 'stress' test, calculating what your payments would be at higher rates of interest to see if you can still service them.

Expect to have to

produce **mountains of paperwork**

if you **work for yourself**

ACTION POINT ➡

REMORTGAGING

You don't have to be moving house to get yourself a good mortgage deal. You could find yourself saving substantial sums of money every month by remortgaging, particularly if you haven't reviewed your mortgage arrangements recently. If you took out your existing loan when the only thing that was on offer was a standard variable rate, you're paying over the odds. You will definitely be able to find yourself a cheaper special deal. And remortgaging is also the most efficient way of freeing up some of the equity built up in your property if you want money for expensive items such as home improvements.

Check out the internet sites reviewed in Web Watch and use the remortgage calculators to work out what you could be paying. Then try approaching your own lender to see if it can match the deal. The market is so cut throat at the moment that it may well agree, assuming you've got a good payment record. Remortgaging with your own lender should be cheaper because it won't need to do as much legal work as if you were starting from scratch with another lender. But if your existing bank or building society won't co-operate, work out if it's worth taking your business elsewhere.

Protecting your mortgage repayments

Taking out life assurance, either with a cheap term assurance policy or through an endowment (see Inside Track, Endowment mortgages – are they a rip off?) will pay off your mortgage if you die. But what happens if you lose your job, have an accident or fall ill so that you can't work? If you aren't earning and can't pay the mortgage every month, you risk getting into arrears and having your property repossessed. State help for mortgage borrowers in financial trouble was drastically scaled back in the early 1990s by the then Conservative government. Even if you qualify for help, you won't get any payouts for the first nine months after making a claim, unless you're claiming on a mortgage taken out before October 1 1995, in which case you wait two months before getting any payout, after which only half your payments are covered for the next four months. Both Conservative and Labour administrations have made it clear they want more people to take out private mortgage payment protection insurance (also known as ASU or accident, sickness and unemployment insurance) through lenders or mortgage brokers, to cover mortgage payments. Costs vary but they'll probably be around £5.50 per £100 of monthly mortgage payments. (So if your mortgage payment is £300, your insurance premium will be £16.50.) However, takeup has been patchy, partly because the insurance is usually set up at the time of taking out the loan, when many borrowers are financially stretched, and partly because some of the policies have had such restrictive conditions that they're hardly worth the paper they're written on. This is an unregulated market but bowing to fierce criticism from consumer groups and ministers, the lending and insurance industries have put together a framework of minimum standards for insurance policies. Check the following:

- Are you covered if you're self-employed?

- If yes, do you have to declare yourself bankrupt before you get a payout?

- Are you covered if a part-time contract is terminated rather than renewed?

- How long do your have to wait after a claim is accepted before your mortgage payments are covered? You shouldn't have to wait more than 60 days.

- Does the policy cover accident, sickness and unemployment?

- Are claims under any one of these headings affected by small print under another?

The Association of British Insurers (**www.abi.org.uk**) and the Council of Mortgage Lenders (**www.cml.org.uk**) have more information.

5

NEW HOMES

BY THE END OF THIS CHAPTER YOU WILL

- Be the bane of the working lives of slickly smiling sales staff handing out glossy brochures at showhomes

- Know what 'offplan' means and think twice before signing up

- Know the difference between a guarantee and a warranty

- Know if you've got the temperament and the energy to build your own dream home

Buying a new home

There's something wickedly seductive about the idea of a new home. Everything is fresh and gleaming, from the paint to the kitchen fittings. No one else's years of limescale are on the bath, the property hasn't been knocked around by generations of DIY enthusiasts whose plumbing and wiring mistakes are just waiting to be discovered. Getting a mortgage should be a piece of cake. Developers claim that many buyers who start off wanting a period house are so taken with new built alternatives that they end up signing up on the spot. Hype, almost certainly, but there's no doubt that buyers are getting less reluctant to consider new homes as developers raise their game and improve their finishes and specifications.

There's something
wickedly seductive

about the idea of a new home

INSIDE TRACK

THE STATE OF PLAY

Property developers have had a good few years after the bloodbath of the early 1990s' recession, particularly in London and the south east where the economy and the housing market have been strong. The Labour government's enthusiasm for regeneration of cities and recycling of brownfield sites has also acted as a catalyst in other major cities including Manchester, Leeds, Liverpool, Cardiff, Bristol and Birmingham, where huge tracts of formerly industrial land and buildings are being converted into trendy lofts and city apartments for well-off empty nesters as well as the young and affluent. The return of such buyers to previously struggling city centres has been a success story and developers are only too keen to respond to calls from ministers and planners for large numbers of 'mixed developments', planning jargon for developments containing shops, offices, restaurants, bars and hotels as well as homes. This kills two birds with one stone, bringing businesses into previously derelict areas and avoiding the emergence of residential ghettos with no facilities. Unfortunately for the less well off, developers are much less enthusiastic about building affordable homes and there are growing fears that many people on modest salaries are being priced out of cities.

Outside the cities, there's a different battle going on as rural areas and the affluent Home Counties alike try to resist pressure from developers to build on greenfield or previously unused sites. At the last estimate, planners calculated that an extra 3.8 million new homes must be built between 1996 and 2021, to cater for the growth in smaller households following divorces and later marriage. The big question is, where will we put all the new homes? The answer, much to the disgust of the Home Counties and south coast, is that a good proportion need to be in the south east, where the jobs are. But available building land here is in short supply, partly because of greenfield and green belt restrictions. If developers do get planning permission, they're under huge pressure to build densely and cheaply, which explains the architecturally charmless, ticky tacky little boxes exploding like malignant growths around so many towns.

The volume property developers argue that they're building what people want, i.e. a pastiche of a period home, built in brick with pitched roof and a few 'features' like contrasting brick or Georgian-style front doors. The architectural purists argue that most people aren't given any choice and that even the glitzy apartment blocks springing up along London's riverside show a dreary lack of imagination.

How the new build buying system works

So you think people only buy homes that physically exist? How wrong you are. If you're planning to buy a new home, you'll probably find yourself making a decision on the basis of a glossy brochure with computer-generated graphics of how the developer hopes your new home will look, a glance round a showflat or showhouse (of which more later) and a tour round a building site. To put it another way, you have little idea of how your home-to-be will look and you're agreeing to pay a large sum of money hoping that it will actually get finished and you'll like it when it's done.

This process is called buying 'offplan' and it's the way the vast majority of speculative developments are now sold, from funky city apartments to exclusive developments of executive homes in the suburbs. This is the only way that developers can make the sums add up. They have already spent time and money buying the land and getting planning permission and now need some commitment from buyers and cashflow in the shape of deposits or downpayments. This is why you drive past a building site and there's a big notice saying '40% reserved/sold', even though there's nothing to see but a big hole in the ground. The busier the market is, the more quickly you have to act. In some parts of London at the height of the most recent boom, you'd have to keep an eye out for land acquired boards and contact the developer immediately, well before marketing started, to have a hope of getting in on the action. In areas which attract lots of buy to let investors, developers often sell off part of a block to big investors before letting the general public in on the secret. If you're in the new property game, here's roughly what to expect:

- You visit a new development, maybe on the strength of a newspaper advertisement or information on the internet (see Web Watch) or because you've seen boards up. Once they start marketing to buyers in general, developers are big advertising spenders, taking out full-page advertisements in the local and national press, erecting banners and billboards, putting up signs to pull in drivers (who may have set out with no intention of buying a property).

- Even if there's nothing to see except earth being churned up by JCBs there will be a sales centre/marketing suite staffed with a couple of bubbly blondes and possibly an eager young man in a suit to add gravitas. The sales centre will be 'tastefully' furnished, with comfortable sofas, low tables and the centrepiece will be a model of the intended development in a glass case. There may be blown-up photographs on the walls extolling the developer's commitment to urban regeneration/building a new community/restoring our heritage. And there could be some slick flat-screen computers loaded with whizzy graphics showing how the new development will look (at least in the developer's imagination).

- You'll be given price lists and glossy brochures. Skip the pages with beautiful couples staring moonily at each other over glasses of wine (of which more later) and turn to the floorplans at the back. This will show the layout and dimensions of the available properties and is almost certainly the most factual information you will receive at this stage. Check especially for odd layouts – rooms opening out of one another, bathrooms and kitchens without natural light (surprisingly common in flats, particularly conversions with awkward shapes). Which way does the property you're interested in face? You'll pay more for views, particularly views over water, which can attract premium prices of up to 20 per cent. But properties on the other side could look over a busy road/railway or even worse into a light well or onto someone else's brick wall. If you're buying a house, look at the overall plan of the development and ask searching questions about how close the houses will be to each other. If answers to your questions aren't forthcoming from the floorplans or overall plans, ask. In the absence of anything physical to see, you could be deciding to spend a lot of money on the basis of this information.

- You're taken to visit the show home. In many developments this has become an art form, designed by interior designers. In some cases, a buyer with more money than time buys the whole thing lock, stock and barrel down to the last bar of soap. But it's easy to be bowled over by sleek minimalist tidiness or the deliberately placed antiques and taken in by some of the tricks of the trade.

- If you fall in love with the development, you can reserve a home on payment of a fee.

- You exchange contracts in the normal way (see Chapter 3) and put down a deposit of between 5 and 10 per cent of the purchase price. But the difference between buying an existing property and a new one is that the length of time between exchange and completion is months or even years, if you're unlucky, rather than weeks. Developers will generally not commit themselves to a specific finishing date although they may specify a month in which you should expect to complete. But a long run of bad weather, problems with labour or materials or other unknowns can all delay completion. The contract will also cover developers in case they have to change materials or finishes, because a supplier goes out of business, for example.

- A long wait between exchanging contracts and committing yourself to the deal and actually moving in can work both ways. In a rising market, you've secured your sale at what seems in retrospect like a bargain price. You could find the value of your property has risen several tens of thousands of pounds by the time you complete. Unfortunately in a falling market you could find that you're stuck with an expensive property with prices falling around you, and the added danger that the developer may go bust and never complete it. This is the risk you take buying a property which doesn't exist.

Often showflats

aren't lit by natural daylight

and a mockup of a view

is pasted onto windows

TRICKS OF THE SHOWHOUSE TRADE

1 *No clutter.* It always makes rooms look bigger if there's nothing but a couple of tasteful artbooks on the coffee table and the dining table isn't spread with the usual family clutter of a broken Thomas the Tank Engine, a forgotten piece of toast and the remains of the Sunday newspapers. Imagine what the same room will look like filled with your book and CD collections and the rest of your possessions.

   ....

2 *Neutral décor.* As in 1, pale, neutral colours make rooms look bigger, which is why developers like them. If this isn't your idea of an exciting colour scheme, will your own scheme make the rooms look unacceptably small?

   ....

3 *Mirrors.* Cleverly created mirrors create an illusion of size. Ditto clever lighting. Often showflats aren't lit by natural daylight and a mockup of a view is pasted onto windows. Rest assured that the view will be the one to be visible from the most expensive flat. But look behind it and you may find a less glamorous outlook of dustbins or brick walls.

   ....

4 *Soundproofing.* Double glazing, heavy curtains and carpets in any rooms where there's no need to show off the trendy hardwood flooring minimise any outside noise.

   ....

5 *Specially built showhome.* If the rest of the development doesn't exist, the showhome sometimes has to be specially built and may be a totally

different place, made out of different materials to what's really going to be on offer. In one London development, the showhome was floating on the canal as the building itself was a shell. The showhome was beautiful but none of the proposed homes would be floating in the same way.

....

6 *'That's stretching it a bit' marketing.* A favourite trick is to fill brochures with pictures of familiar famous and beautiful sites implying that the development is close by. Often it isn't at all but many buyers are taken in.

....

WEB WATCH

➡ Most developers have their own websites, similar to those of estate agents, with details and pictures of their developments. Also worth checking out are websites which specialize in new homes.

➡ www.freeagents.co.uk

Background: Founded by a property journalist with venture capital.

Claim: Contains details of 40,000 new homes in London and the south east, specializing in quality 'niche' properties.

How it works: You search by postcode or click on a map of the regions the site covers, including London, the Home Counties and the south coast. The search shows up not just developments in your specified postcode but also in surrounding postcodes which can be useful as postcode areas are fairly narrowly drawn. Alongside the property search facility, you can get postcode-specific information about state and independent schools in the area. You can also order reports on the environmental quality of your postcode area, including pollution and flood risk data, at a cost of £3.50 and have them emailed to you within 48 hours. Click on Links for one of the most comprehensive lists of useful property-related websites in the business, with everything from finance to removals and utilities companies (although critics may argue that it would be a good idea to remove defunct websites like netmortgage from the listing).

Pros: Clear, easy-to-use pages with most of the major developers in London and the south east represented, including Berkeley Homes, Bellway Homes and Bryant Homes.

Cons: No direct postcode-related link between the property search section and the schools search section, so that you have to start from scratch inputting your postcode again for details of schools.

Verdict: Worth a visit.

➡ **www.newhomesnetwork.co.uk**

Claim: 'The easiest and quickest solution to finding your dream property.'

How it works: You have to register to get access to the new homes database but it's worth it if you're outside London because it carries information on new developments from Land's End to John O'Groats (or at least the south west to Scotland). Most major developers are represented including Barratt Homes, Crest Nicholson, Laing Homes, Wilcon Homes and Fairview New Homes. Drop-down menus give you a choice of searching by area or by developer, with settings for maximum prices.

There's also a home store facility where you can store property information for future reference or email information to friends and family.

Pros: Simple and quick to use.

Cons: No obvious way of refining searches to narrow down area-based listings. So in London you get lists of every development in places you wouldn't be seen dead in, in no particular order.

Verdict: Comprehensive but search engine doesn't do its database justice.

➡ Other sites with more limited new homes databases include **www.fish4.co.uk** (see Chapter 1)

DID YOU KNOW?

If you're moving to a new house and want to sell your own home quickly, the developer may take your current home in part-exchange and sell it on for you. The advantage of this is that your existing property is taken off your hands and sold at a price based on 95 per cent of the market value calculated from the average of two or three independent valuations. The argument for the 5 per cent reduction in market value is that you're saving on agents' fees. You'd normally have to be trading up to your new property, buying a new home from a developer which is at least 30 per cent more expensive than your old one. Developers who offer this facility on selected developments include Fairview New Homes (**www.fairview.co.uk**) and Barratt Homes (**www.barratthomes.co.uk**). Depending on the state of the market and how much competition there is for buyers, you may be offered the full market value of your home. You may also be offered incentives including help with your deposit, legal fees and stamp duty paid, or cashback, a sum of money paid to you on completion. The worse the state of the property market, the more incentives developers will offer you. This isn't altruism on their part – they want to get rid of properties quickly and get your money in their pockets.

The selling of a lifestyle – is it you?

The word 'lifestyle' is one of the most used and abused words in new homes marketing. Like a lot of marketing, developers' brochures and blurb are designed to appeal to the inner aspirations of potential buyers. The core message is that this development is no mere arrangement of bricks and mortar but the key to a New You. City apartments are sold with underground carparks (your car is so flashy that you can't risk leaving it in the street), porterage (there are some very high profile people living in the block who need 24-hour protection even if it's just help getting back into their apartment when they've lost their keys) and gyms (you slave at your desk all day in a high powered job moving billions of pounds across the world in seconds and need to work off your adrenalin). Surburban neo-Georgian piles have names from Olde English counties or reassuringly classy towns like Winchester and project a lifestyle of Joanna Trollope-style country living (even if you catch the 7.30 to Waterloo every morning).

Great, if this is what you really want. But be honest with yourself. Do you really want to pay high service charges (set aside several thousand pounds a year) for a gym you may never use, porters you don't need and a car parking space if you don't need a car? If you want to live in the country, is a suburban pile really the answer to your prayers or could you find an existing property which provides the same space, with more charm, for less money or even build your own? Remember, new homes come at premium prices.

Alongside the New You message in new homes advertising runs a parallel message that you're buying an individual, unique property (even though it's exactly like hundreds of others). Specifications are certainly higher than they used to be but developers, particularly at the lower end of the market, install hundreds of identical fixtures and fittings taking maximum advantage of volume discounts from suppliers. If you don't want to go round to your neighbour's for a quick drink after work and think you're in the wrong house, head more upmarket if you can afford it and choose one of the growing number of developers offering a choice of bathrooms, kitchens, curtains and carpets. If you've reserved a property at an early stage in building, you may also be able to customize your new

New homes
come at premium prices

home, even changing parts of the layout to suit you or doing a deal to build an extra room or conservatory.

It's a warranty, not a guarantee

One of the best things about buying a new home is that maintenance bills should be low, at least in the first few years. Most buyers would argue that it's reasonable to expect a house that's just been built and inspected to be structurally sound, weatherproof and fully functioning, down to the last kitchen tap and lavatory flush.

But, unfortunately, it's never that simple with property and there are many reports of shoddy workmanship ranging from the substandard to the downright dangerous. According to Chris Lorentzen, who set up the Association of New Homeowners (Nanho **www.nanho.org.uk**) after experiencing structural problems with his own new home, complaints to his organization have nearly doubled in the past two years to 12,000. And these aren't in the dripping tap league. Problems include inadequate foundations, faulty drains, defective structural timbers, weak mortar and houses not laid out according to the plans, a big drawback if you're buying offplan. Growing pressure for developers to build on brownfield sites has resulted in serious defects where houses are built on buried rubbish or sites at risk of flooding, claims Lorentzen.

Buyers are frequently lulled into a false sense of security by developers offering a 10-year warranty against major structural defects and not explaining clearly that the warranty is *not* a guarantee. Some new homes advertising even misleading describes a warranty as a guarantee. Many people are so confident that the structure of their property is guaranteed that they do not bother to have a structural survey (see Chapter 3 for details of the different kinds of surveys).

The National House Building Council (NHBC, **www.nhbc.co.uk**) has the lion's share of the structural defects warranty market with its Buildmark policy. The other player in the market is Zurich Municipal (**www.zurich.co.uk**), which offers similar cover. But both companies are *insurance* companies and the warranties are insurance policies. They will only pay out on claims which meet their criteria. These can be so narrowly drawn that as one critic says: 'Your house has to be almost falling down before you receive a payout.'

These are the main points to bear in mind when buying a new property with an NHBC warranty:

- NHBC acts as a regulator to the building industry, is an approved building inspector and issues insurance cover to its developer members who sell it on as part of a new home package to you.

- The structural defects warranty lasts for 10 years. But if defects appear in the first two years you must approach the builder responsible before contacting your local NHBC office.

- If your builder has gone out of business (not an unusual occurrence in such a notoriously boom and bust industry), NHBC will step in and cover you *if* the defect is covered under the policy.

- If the builder refuses to co-operate, NHBC runs an arbitration scheme. Growing numbers of homeowners are having to turn to NHBC after builders refuse to correct problems. In 1999–2000, 6531 had such problems, says the NHBC, compared with 5230 in 1998–1999. NHBC found in favour of homeowners in 60 per cent of cases.

- The Buildmark policy covers claims for major structural defects, defined as damage which will cost £500 or more to put right. Under pressure from homeowners, this cover was extended last year to cover defects in ceilings, in internal non-load-bearing walls and staircases and debonding of plaster (where plaster comes unstuck from the wall). Other earlier extensions of the cover include failures in double glazing and the cost to homeowners of remediating contaminated land.

So before you commit yourself to buying a new home, here are some top tips from the Royal Institution of Chartered Surveyors:

- Check the brickwork and paintwork. Does it look right and is it clean and even?

- Are the windows and doors property fitted into the walls?

- Does the floor shake if you stand in a room, raise yourself on tiptoe and lower your weight onto your heels?

- Can you hear people walking around upstairs?

- Open and shut the windows to check whether they stick.

- These or other obvious defects could be a sign that the whole house is shoddy.

- If problems start after you move in (dripping taps, leaking loos or pipes for example) keep a detailed diary which will help you if you have to make a claim.

- New homes have to be 'run in' just like car engines used to be. They contain up to 1500 gallons of water in plaster and other materials and you should keep the temperature in the house as even as possible to prevent excessive drying out and cracking.

Self build – can you face it?

What if you're keen to buy a new house but just can't find what you want? You can compromise – or you can build your own. This option

What if you're keen

to buy a new house

but just can't find

what you want?

isn't for the fainthearted. You need to be the calm, organized type who can face the prospect of living for months or even years on a building site, keeping track directly or indirectly of the activities of a bevy of builders, carpenters, electricians, plumbers and roofers. But it means you get exactly the house you want, where you want. And it usually works out cheaper than buying through a developer, even buying the land, because you avoid the developer's markup of between 25 and 30 per cent.

Finding the right plot of land is often the most challenging part of the whole exercise, particularly in London and the south east where land is scarce and expensive and people can take up to a year to find a suitable plot. The internet is becoming an increasingly valuable resource for information on land for sale, supplies, services (solicitors, surveyors, architects and so on) and finance.

WEB WATCH

➡ Check out the following:

➡ **www.homebuilding.co.uk**

Background: Run by the publishers of *Homebuilding and Renovation* magazine, the leading monthly glossy magazine for homebuilders.

Claim: Information updated daily.

How it works: A magazine-style site with plenty of articles, access to back issues, beginners' guide and a self build discussion forum where registered users can discuss anything from planning headaches to gripes about individual building products. You can also link to **www.plotfinder.net**, *H & R*'s recently established database of land for sale and houses to renovate. Plotfinder has a free demo with drop-down menus so that you can click on the counties you're interested in for details of land in those counties. If you want to register as a user, it's £35 for a one-year subscription to the land database for three counties.

➡ www.buildstore.co.uk

Background: Owned by a group of venture capitalists, individuals and companies involved in the self build market, including Potton, the timber-frame homes manufacturer.

Claim: 'The complete service for self builders.'

How it works: Editorial features include Why Self Build? (Because you can build what you like, where you like and save money in the process). There's an A–Z of suppliers with links and My Project allows you to keep track of mortgage applications, order materials and manage projects online. The site's Plotshare service maintains the National Building Plot Register of 5000 plots of land for sale accessed by county and matches self builders who want to share land costs. Registration to Plotsearch costs £39 for a lifetime's subscription and unlimited access to the database for three counties. An extra £10 gives you access to Plotshare where you can team up with others to buy land you can't afford on your own.

➡ www.ebuild.co.uk

Background: Published by specialist publishers Webguides Online.

Claim: Independent from trade magazines and the building trade.

How it works: The site includes a directory of suppliers from architectural salvage to waste disposal with links to useful sites; discussion boards for chats with other builders and free advertising of land and plots for sale.

➡ www.npbs.co.uk

Background: The site of the Norwich and Peterborough Building Society.

How it works: Mortgages for self build projects are a niche market because the money is released in stages. Norwich and Peterborough is a keen enthusiast of the self build market with several self builders on its staff including the general manager. The site includes advice for self builders and an example of a typical self build mortgage. The loan is released in stages, starting with up to 85 per cent of the value of the land. Funds for building costs are paid in stages: 15 per cent when foundations and damp proof course are complete; 15 per cent at first-floor joist level; 15 per cent at wall plate level; 20 per cent when the roof is on; 15 per cent when plastering is done and 20 per cent when the property is finished.

6

MOVING HOUSE AND HOME IMPROVEMENTS

BY THE END OF THIS CHAPTER YOU WILL

- Consider renouncing material possessions for ever and joining a religious order

- Vow never to volunteer to pack the kitchen cupboards again

- Understand the value of the Royal Mail's post redirection service

Planning your moving arrangements

By this stage in the game, you will almost certainly have exhausted your emotional energy, not to mention your finances, in the process of buying your new home and getting both sides committed to the sale by exchanging contracts. Making any moving arrangements before exchanging contracts may seem like tempting fate. But you may only have a couple of weeks between exchanging contracts and completing the sale, and the more tasks you leave until the last minute the more stressful it will be.

A suggested completion date will have been set at the beginning of the whole process, when your offer is accepted and the seller's solicitor starts drawing up a draft contract, which has to include a completion date. But, housebuying being the chaotic process that it is, dates which seemed ridiculously far away when first agreed soon look terrifyingly close. An extra week for structural reports, delays and negotiations with lenders on loans, last minute arguments with the other side about what is or isn't included in the price and a breakdown somewhere along the line in the buying chain are just some of the commonest causes of delays.

So it's the rule rather than the exception that dates are pushed back and draft contracts amended accordingly. Only when contracts have been exchanged is the completion date set in stone, on pain of expensive legal action if you don't produce the money for your new home and move out of your old one on the appointed day. But if there have been long delays

By this stage in the game, you will almost **certainly exhausted** have **your emotional energy** to exchange and everyone's getting desperate to finalize the deal, you could come under pressure to complete quickly. Or you could want to force the pace yourself, particularly if you have to fit in with school terms or other commitments. This can mean a huge last minute rush, so start organizing the logistics of your move as early as possible.

Warning: It's tempting to set completion for a Friday so that you have the weekend to unpack (or more likely collapse with a few stiff drinks). But lots of other people have the same idea. It's the busiest day of the week for removal firms. If there's a big chain of buyers and sellers all trying to complete on the same day, there's also a risk you may not get all the money transferred before banks shut up shop for the weekend and solicitors clock off. And if you haven't been efficient about informing electricity, gas and phone companies of your move, you may find yourself facing a cold, dark, silent welcome, with all services cut off, unable to be reinstated until the following week, possibly on pain of a reconnection charge.

DID YOU KNOW?

One way of avoiding the going for broke, 'let's all complete now' scenario is to complete the purchase of your new property a couple of days before selling your existing one. This gives you time to sort out urgent tasks (getting carpets, kitchen equipment and so on installed), getting services connected, cleaning the new house before putting your possessions in. But the glaring problem with this approach, as you will doubtless have spotted, is that you will still own your old property. If both properties are mortgaged and you haven't yet redeemed the mortgage on your current home by completing the sale, you'll have to take out a bridging loan. There are two types of bridging loan. A closed loan is one where you've exchanged contracts and both sides are committed to the deal. This is relatively low risk for the lender, who knows the deal will go through and just has to advance you your new loan to tide you over for a couple of days. Much more risky (and more expensive for you) is an open bridging loan, where you're not yet committed to the deal and there's no final firm date for completion. You'll pay at least 2 per cent over the going standard variable rate (see Chapter 4) for an open bridging loan. And there are no fixed rates, so if interest rates rise, so do your mortgage payments on your new property, while at the same time you're still paying the bills on your old one. When government ministers were casting round for ways of speeding up the housebuying process in the late 1990s, one of the ideas they came up with was a new type of 'chainbreaker' bridging loan, allowing people to free themselves from long housing chains. But lenders have been unenthusiastic about such loans since many people came a cropper in the downturn of the early 1990s and little has been heard of the plan since.

Alternatively, if you can't face selling and buying at the same time and don't want to take out a bridging loan, you can sell your existing home, put your furniture in storage and move into rented accommodation until you find somewhere you want to buy. The advantage of this is that you've got the money from selling sitting in the bank so that you can move quickly when the right place comes up. But it means more upheaval with an interim move, and rental and storage costs add up.

Your main tasks

However you choose to time your move, these are your core tasks:

- finalize removal/storage arrangements
- contact electricity/gas/phone/cable companies and other utilities to tell them your moving date
- organize your funds so that you can transfer all remaining money needed to complete the sale into your solicitor's account, for him/her to pay to your seller's solicitor.

Removals

The big question is: get a removal firm in or do it yourself?

DIY moves

Pros

- It's cheaper, especially if you've hardly any possessions or big furniture, you can call on a team of strong, willing friends and you're not moving far away. Your only cost is hiring a van, plus petrol, plus goods in transit insurance cover if you want.

Cons

- You almost certainly have a lot more stuff than you think. Have you looked in your attic recently? Or your loft? Or the garden shed? How many books/CDs/pictures have you got? What's in your kitchen cupboards? And when did you last weed out your wardrobe? A DIY move means packing all this and carrying it physically into a van, unloading it at the other end and putting it in the new property, with possibly a long drive in an unfamiliar van in between.
- Stairs, doorways and passageways are more awkwardly shaped than you would ever have believed possible.
- Supermarkets and shops have a limited supply of usefully shaped boxes for packing, however helpful the supermarket shelf stackers are

Stairs, doorways and passageways are
more awkwardly shaped than

you would ever have believed possible

about saving you empty boxes. Allow several weeks to collect up enough boxes to store the contents of even a modest home. At the end of it you'll know everyone in the local supermarket by their first names but so what if you're moving away? Alternatively, if you're prepared to pay for packaging, the Big Yellow Self-Storage chain of shops has branches in London and the south east open seven days a week. You can order goods online at **www.thebigyellow.co.uk** including storage packs, boxes, bubble wrap and packing tape.

Professional removers

Pros

- They know (or should know) what they're doing when lifting heavy furniture, negotiating tricky doorways and dismantling items temporarily to get them into the house. Use a firm which is a member of the British Association of Removers (BAR, **www.bar.co.uk**), the removal men's professional body. Members have to adhere to a code of professional practice, meet minimum standards and provide emergency service and finance guarantees. There's also a conciliation scheme if you not satisfied with the service.

- Removers can offer various levels of packing services. The most expensive option is for the removers to pack everything. The second most expensive is for them to pack the breakable and fiddly things like crockery and glass. The cheapest way to employ removers is to get them to provide chests and boxes in advance for you to pack your own possessions in the day before the move. If you really want deluxe treatment you can get them to unpack everything at the other end as well, although this means you have to be mega organized and know where you want everything to go in your new house.

Cons

- Professional removers are more expensive than doing it yourself.

If you're going for the professional option:

- Get two or three estimates. You can find names of local firms through the British Association of Removers (BAR, **www.bar.co.uk**), through the Yellow Pages (**www.yell.com**) or through Thomson Local Directories (**www.thomweb.co.uk**).

- There are also growing numbers of property websites which include quotes from removal firms (see Web Watch).

- You should expect estimators to go through your whole house and garden, including lofts, cellars and that cupboard into which you've chucked everything that you can't find a place for elsewhere.

- Check whether your possessions will be covered by your household contents insurance policy, and extend the cover if they aren't.

- Don't wait until you've exchanged contracts to organize removers, especially if there'll only be a week or two between exchange and completion. If no one can fit you in on your agreed moving day, you'll be stuck.

WEB WATCH

➡ The internet lends itself well to getting quotes and establishing ballpark prices for everything to do with homebuying, including removals. Log onto the following:

➡**www.reallymoving.com**

Background: Launched at the end of 1999.

Claim: An independent, privately financed site, 'the leading provider of online home moving services'.

How it works: A one-stop shop site linked to Propertyfinder (see Chapter 1) for property searches and upmystreet (see Chapter 1) for local area information. But reallymoving's speciality is online quotation services for removals and utilities companies. Registering will get you three quotes for each of removers, solicitors, surveyors and utilities companies, either online immediately or by email. There's also a Minimove facility for people who haven't got enough stuff to fill a van and want to find someone to share removal costs with. Editorially, there's a brief guide to moving and a useful planner laid out graphically showing what you should do when during the period between exchange and completion. Once in your new home, there's a directory of links to everything for the home and garden from gardening tools to sofa beds.

Pros: Easy and clear to use.

Cons: Quotes are limited to reallymoving's partners, which in the case of utilities number just one, so making comparison difficult.

Verdict: Generally useful site. Used by other sites, like **www.ihavemoved.com**, to provide quotation services.

Contact utilities

A dull but vital task is to contact all the companies which provide you with electricity, gas, telephones and cable TV and tell them you're moving. It's better to wait until you've exchanged contracts so that you don't have to change the information you've originally given and risk administrative chaos. But do it as soon as possible after exchange because you have to organize meter readings at your old property on the day you move out. You may be allowed to do this yourself but electricity companies in particular seem to prefer to send someone along and you need to co-ordinate this along with a hundred other moving day tasks (telling removal men what to take and what to leave, making yet another five cups of tea, winding up the Old MacDonald music box again to keep the baby quiet).

WEB WATCH

➡ Most utilities will ask for confirmation of your new address and moving date in writing. If you can't face doing this, log onto:

➡www.ihavemoved.com

Background: Started 1999, backed by consortium of investors and industry figures.

Claim: 'The UK's first free online change of address service.'

How it works: You register, enter your old and new addresses and the companies you want to notify, supply account numbers and meter readings where relevant and ihavemoved sends the information to the companies. The process takes about 15 minutes, the site claims. There's a useful reminder list of all the companies and organizations you should be sending change of address notifications to, including the obscure ones you always forget such as insurance companies, magazines subscriptions departments and alumni associations. The site is funded by companies keen to keep track of their customers rather than lose them to a competitor in these dog-eat-dog post-nationalized utilities days. A quotation service for removers, solicitors, surveyors and so on is provided by reallymoving.com (see earlier).

Pros: Easy to use with explanations and demonstrations of how the site works.

Cons: Layout is a bit texty and messy.

Verdict: A brilliantly simple idea for which householders across the nation should be grateful.

➡www.simplymove.co.uk

Background: Conceived August 1998 but only got off the ground more recently.

Claim: 'Our aim is to make some of the more tedious tasks [of housemoving] as simple as filling in a form.'

How it works: You register, provide old and new addresses, account details and so on and simplymove notifies the utilities companies. It provides pre-printed stationery with your new address to notify friends and family. You can fill in details of moving dates on the site and adjust them as necessary.

DID YOU KNOW?

However punctilious you try to be with change of address notifications, some will inevitably fall through the net. So it's worth paying for the redirection service operated by Royal Mail (**www.royalmail.com**). You can have mail redirected for up to two years over periods of one month, three months, six months or 12 months. Current costs are £12.60, £21, £42 and £63 respectively. You need to apply five days before you want the redirection to start. You can get forms from your local post office or download one from the internet.

Home improvements

Homebuyers fall into three rough camps. The first lot want to move straight into a property which needs no work. They're looking for minimum hassle and don't want to do anything more strenuous than change a lightbulb. The second lot think 'We could fit a great new kitchen/bathroom/conservatory/loft extension' and never quite get round to it before they move again. And the third lot are home improvers, dedicated watchers of makeover and interior design programmes and readers of property supplements and readers' mailbags on the intricacies of planning permission, damp proofing and dry rot. They keep DIY stores in business and builders busy. They do not only the dull but necessary jobs like mending the roof and repointing brickwork but also the high profile stuff like loft and kitchen extensions and conservatories.

The home improvers **keep**

DIY stores **in business**
and builders busy

TOP OF THE HOME IMPROVEMENT POPS

According to the most recent annual home improvements survey from the Halifax, the UK's largest mortgage lender, our favourite home improvements in order overall are:

1 double glazing

2 fitted kitchen

3 garden improvements

4 new bathroom

5 home security.

Nearly 40 per cent of Halifax customers had made some sort of improvement to their properties in the last 12 months, spending on average between £2000 and £4000.

Growing numbers of people are carrying out improvements in the hope that it will help sell their homes, rating double glazing, central heating, fitted kitchen, garage and new bathroom (in that order) most likely to pull in the punters.

And they're pretty spot on, judging by the items homebuyers deem necessities. Central heating is top, named by 75 per cent of respondents, followed by garden, double glazing, fitted kitchen, garage and modern bathroom. But don't pull out all the stops to install a new bathroom if your main priority is to sell your home on quickly – buyers rate this as a luxury less important than a conservatory, home security, garden improvements, energy-saving devices or a fitted bedroom.

But valuers warn that many home improvers are over-optimistic about how much value improvements will add to a property, especially if you're planning to do it up and move on. The advice from the Halifax is that:

- you'll recoup all your outlay immediately if you install central heating or build a garage as these features are most sought after by homebuyers. Central heating in particular isn't that expensive to install but any buyer will recoil at the upheaval of carrying out the work and will pay a higher price for a property that already has central heating.

- you'll recoup a proportion of your outlay on new kitchens, house extensions, loft conversions, double glazing or replacement windows, improvements to the bathroom or adding a new bathroom/WC.

- the following make your property more saleable without necessarily allowing you to recoup your outlay: conservatory, leisure facilities, garden landscaping.

As a general rule, elaborate and expensive home improvements such as extensions and conservatories are best done because you're planning to live in your home for a while and you want to enjoy the improvements yourself. The moneyspinners are the smaller, less glamorous improvements which growing numbers of people in our affluent society regard as necessities, like central heating, (although only 75 per cent of Halifax customers rated central heating as top necessity – the other 25 per cent must be a hardy lot up there in the Pennines.)

But a lot depends on the size of the property, its type, its location and its existing value. If you've just bought a Victorian terrace in a suburb of a city like Manchester or Leeds where a £30,000 house is an expensive house, there's no point installing a state of the art kitchen costing as much again. You'll

Central heating and **double glazing**
may make **your property**
more saleable as well as warmer
for you to live in

never get your money back because every street has an unspoken price
'ceiling'. Buyers won't pay more than a certain amount for properties in that
area. But central heating and double glazing may make your property more
saleable as well as warmer for you to live in. By contrast, in expensive family
areas of London, large family kitchens with lots of shiny work surfaces,
conservatories opening up the back of a large Victorian or Edwardian house or
loft conversions providing extra space for children and teenagers are big
sellers and you should recoup your money, particularly in a boom market. In
the late 1990s, Wandsworth council in south west London saw a huge surge in
planning applications for conservatories as they became the latest 'nappy
valley' accessory.

Planning matters

When you move into your new home, you'll be full of plans for
everything from how to arrange the furniture to how you're going to use
the loft space, build a garage on the redundant space between the house
and the fence and generally put your own stamp on it.

But planning laws governing what you can and can't do with your
property are complex and vary depending on how different local councils
interpret the legislation. Homeowners can and do ignore the rules with
impunity and some get away with it. But the ultimate penalty for

breaching the rules is to be ordered to knock down whatever you've built and reinstate your property as it was. Even if you don't need planning permission (and in a number of circumstances you don't, see below), any extension, conversion, knocking of two rooms into one or other structural alterations will almost certainly need to be signed off by the local authority building inspector. Not being able to produce this paperwork could cause problems when you come to sell.

Do you need planning permission?

You can never say never, if you're dealing with local planning departments. But generally you won't need planning permission for:

- extensions that are 15 per cent or less of the original size of a detached or semi-detached house or 10 per cent of the original size of a terrace, up to a maximum of 115 cubic metres. Extensions mustn't stick out beyond the front wall of the house

- sheds, greenhouses or garages which cover 50 per cent or less of the garden and are five metres high or lower.

- fences and walls less than one metre high at the front and two metres high elsewhere.

A good builder or architect will know what you do or don't need permission for and local firms should be familiar with the idiosyncracies of the local council. Word of mouth is usually the best way to find architects or builders. Alternatively, the Clients Advisory Service of the Royal Institute of British Architects (**www.architecture.com**) can give you a list of suitable architects locally.

Conservation areas

If you're in a conservation area (your local searches and your seller's answers to standard questions will have told you if you are), the rules are a bit tighter, although there are certain 'permitted development rights' for householders in most conservation areas.

You shouldn't need permission for:

- extensions, sheds and fences as long as they conform to the specifications just referred to
- replacing windows and doors with modern alternatives
- porches, providing they comply with specific proportions and distances.

But you *will* need permission for:

- stone cladding, pebbledash or rendering
- satellite dishes
- dormer windows.

There are some exceptions to these rules:

- If you're in a flat, you have to get planning permission for any alteration. The reason for this is that it's easier to block someone's light or invade someone's privacy than it is in a house. As many city streets will testify, it's also easier in multiply occupied properties for a 'domino effect' to build up as one flatowner adds a satellite dish and another copies him, thinking it must be alright if the neighbours are doing it. As flats are almost always leasehold (see Chapter 3) any changes you make will also be governed by the terms of your lease and you'll need to get permission from the freeholder.

- Local authorities have the power to impose tighter rules on areas they believe to be at risk. If you're in an area covered by a so called Article 4 direction, you will almost certainly have to get planning permission for any alterations.

What about ex-Council property?

Listed buildings

Listed buildings are by definition unusual/historic/beautiful so can be a tempting proposition. But be warned if you've bought a historic wreck to restore: alterations are so tightly controlled that some homeowners end up thinking listed buildings are more trouble than they're worth.

The following are listed:

- all buildings dating from before 1700 and most from before 1840 if they survive in anything like their original state
- buildings of exceptional character post-1840
- selected buildings post-1914.

Buildings are graded I (3 per cent of all listed structures, mostly churches and public buildings), II' (5 per cent) and II (92 per cent, including most domestic properties). Call the Listed Buildings Information Service on 020 7208 8221 to check if a building is listed.

You need listed building consent for demolishing, extending or altering any listed building externally or internally. English Heritage must be informed of plans for grade I and II' buildings and of demolitions for grade II buildings.

You could face an unlimited fine or up to a year in prison for carrying out unauthorized works to listed buildings. You may be able to get a grant from English Heritage for up to 60 per cent of listed building works costing £10,000 or more although new owners don't normally qualify.

You could face an **unlimited fine or up to a year in prison** for carrying out unauthorized works to listed buildings

Local authorities sometimes offer limited grants of a few thousand pounds. The Society for the Protection of Ancient Buildings (SPAB, **www.spab.org.uk**) has technical information sheets on the restoration of old houses using traditional materials.

ACTION POINT ➡

Fancy buying up a historic wreck and restoring it to its former glory? SPAB keeps a quarterly list of about 200 properties for sale which you will receive as a member of SPAB (membership fee £24 a year). Check out also SAVE Britain's Heritage (**www.savebritainsheritage.org**), which has a register of buildings at risk for sale in England and Wales excluding London. For the register of listed buildings at risk in London and grade I and II' listed buildings across the country go to English Heritage at **www.english-heritage.org.uk**.

7

RENTING AND

LETTING

BY THE END OF THIS CHAPTER TENANTS WILL

- Vow to develop a strong sense of smell (to check for damp and carbon monoxide poisoning)

- Be picky about who they write out deposit cheques to

- Realize they have more legal rights than you thought possible

LANDLORDS WILL

- Realize that what the much misunderstood Peter Rachman was trying to demonstrate when he brought his heavies round to a damp slum in Notting Hill was that there is a direct relationship between rental income and landlord expenditure on maintenance and repairs

- Make sure that the neutral colour section of the paint card is the most well thumbed.

Renting

If you live in a rented home, you're in a minority. Such is the British obsession with homeownership that nearly 70 per cent of us own our own homes, with only 30 per cent renting privately, through the council or through a social landlord like a housing association. Just 11 per cent of people live in privately rented accommodation. Most people see renting as a temporary option, until they 'settle down' and 'get a place of their own'. Renting is second best, redolent of 'The Young Ones' – student digs and sleezy basements to let for extortionate rents. For many would-be tenants, the most telling argument against renting and in favour of buying is that with mortgage rates currently so low, it's cheaper to buy than rent, as long as you can get enough money together upfront for a deposit and moving costs (see Chapter 3).

But renting is worth considering, particularly if you move around a lot or just want to test out an area to see if you like living there. Estate agents across the country say a good proportion of their purchasers are already renting locally. And the general standard of privately rented properties has improved dramatically over the last 10 years, thanks to new laws which allow landlords to charge market rents and get their homes back more easily (see A Bit of History). Tenants' rights groups may argue that

Such is the **British obsession with homeownership** that nearly

70 per cent of us own our own homes

the Housing Act 1988, which brought in these significant changes, amounts to a landlord's charter but most landlords won't invest in repairs, maintenance and decent fixtures and fittings unless they can make a profit or at least break even.

INSIDE TRACK

A BIT OF HISTORY

At the beginning of the twentieth century only the very wealthy owned their own homes. The vast majority lived in privately rented flats. (Councils weren't yet the big landlords they would become post-1945.) Rents were artificially controlled, following a government clampdown on landlord profiteering during the Great War, creating a big disincentive for landlords to carry out repairs.

But homeownership started to become a realistic alternative in the building booms of the 1920s and 1930s, when millions of new homes were built around new transport links and cheap mortgage finance became available to the middle classes, lured to the suburbs with the promise of domestic bliss just a metropolitan tube ride away from town.

In 1957, the then Conservative government introduced new laws to decontrol rents for new tenancies, to encourage landlords to carry out repairs and invest in more properties to let, against the background of a continuing housing shortage. This was the signal for unscrupulous landlords like the notorious Peter Rachman to try and winkle out existing tenants on controlled rents so that they could let out their properties again at higher rents. Revelations of widespread tenant abuse led to a government clampdown and a partial return to controlled rents, leading many landlords to sell out to their sitting tenants rather than continue in the letting business.

This exacerbated the already chronic shortage of properties to rent, forcing many people who would have preferred to be tenants onto the housing ladder. Home ownership for those who could afford to buy was becoming a moneyspinner as homeowners saw the value of their homes rocket, thanks to

Landlords and tenants

aren't supposed to like each other

high inflation. By the late 1980s, 'getting on the property ladder' was the name of the game, credit was easy and lenders weighed in, handing out mortgages to all comers. Even council tenants were allowed in on the bonanza, earning the right to buy their council homes at massively discounted prices. Renting was uncool, something only for students and the desperate.

But renting started to look distinctly attractive in the downturn of the 1990s, as millions of homeowners saw the value of their homes tumble and others were trapped in negative equity, unable to sell (see Chapter 4). Demand for property to rent was stronger than it had been for decades among young professional people unnerved by falling prices and high mortgage rates.

And a new breed of landlord started to spring up to cater for middle-class demand, thanks to new laws introduced in 1989 which created a new type of tenancy, the assured shorthold. For the first time, landlords could let their properties at market rents fixed only for the term of the current tenancy (normally six months to start with) and get tenants out at the end of this time as a matter of course, instead of having to fight protracted battles through the courts (see later). Mortgage lenders responded to demand for buy to let properties with more competitive loan rates. Cash investors have also been active in the buy to let market during the recent boom, many investing the proceeds of large city bonuses in bricks and mortar. Not all buy to let investors have made a packet, having bought in the wrong place at the wrong time (see Buy to Let). But others have played the property market cannily enough to see good capital growth as well as a steady rental income from their property portfolios. For tenants, the buy to let landlord has meant an increase in supply and a discernible improvement in standards.

Landlords versus tenants

Landlords and tenants aren't supposed to like each other. Press coverage of renting centres on conflicts between the two sides, landlords and tenants from hell, non-payment of rent, wrecked properties and landlord heavies chucking pregnant women onto the street. But unfortunately, unlike buyers and sellers who never have to see each other again once they've sealed the deal, the signing of a tenancy agreement marks the beginning of a relationship rather than the end. If you're a tenant, you want a decently fitted, safe property which you can treat as your home, while respecting the fact that it's someone else's. If you're a landlord, you want someone who takes care of your home, pays the rent on time and leaves promptly through mutual agreement. Both sides are more likely to achieve their aims if they play straight with each other.

This chapter looks first at renting from the tenant's point of view, then at letting from the landlord's side.

Tenants

Starting your search

You're new in town. You don't want to commit yourself to buying, or can't afford to just yet. You've sold your current home and plan to rent until you find the right home to buy. You've been relocated for a couple of years and don't want to get embroiled in buying. All these are strong reasons for renting. So where do you start? As with buying (see Chapter 1), begin by deciding on your priorities, to narrow down your search. Of course you can always move after six months if you discover you've made a mistake and don't want to renew your tenancy. But unless you want regular upheavals and removal costs, it pays to think your search through:

- *What sort of property do you want?* (This sounds basic but it's a fundamental starting point.) Are you happy with a room in a shared house (the cheapest option)? Or do you want to pay more for a self-contained flat or house? Do you want to share with a friend or live alone?

- *Do you want furnished or unfurnished accommodation?* Unfurnished is an option for homeowners between homes who want to use their own furniture rather than storing it and for relocators, if they're planning to stay several years. Unfurnished properties are becoming more popular with landlords, thanks in part to much stricter regulations governing fire safety regulations for furniture (see Landlord's obligations). Furnished is the practical option for young people just starting out, whose purchasing priorities to date almost certainly haven't included a three-piece suite and a dinner service. Whether it's furnished or unfurnished, you should expect a fitted kitchen and bathroom, carpets, curtains and electrical fittings to be provided.

- *Get an idea of prices in areas you're interested in.* There's no point wasting time looking in places you can't afford. Look in newspapers, lettings agents' windows and on the internet (see Web Watch) to refine your search.

- *If it's a flat, which floors do you prefer?* Younger people may be happy to climb several flights of stairs every time they come back from the shops but this is an unappealing prospect if you're armed with a buggy and young children. Similarly, basement and ground floor flats aren't always popular with single women, for security reasons.

- *If you're looking for a family home, do you need to be in a specific catchment area for schools?* If so, make sure you get information on the catchment limits from the school directly, rather than relying on what could be out-of-date knowledge from a lettings agent.

- *Check out bus and train routes.* Do you need to commute to work? If so, which station(s) are most convenient and how far are you prepared to walk to get there? The most sought after properties tend to be no more than 10 minutes' walk from a well-served station, but you'll pay more for the privilege. If your budget's tight, can you face a 15- or 20-minute walk every morning or evening?

Rents

What to look for

There's no hard and fast rule about how rents are calculated and quoted. The two key questions are:

- *Weekly or monthly?* This depends where you're looking. To put it baldly, the posher the area, the more likely you are to be quoted a weekly rent (because you're less likely to faint with horror when you first see the rent written down). Cheaper areas are more likely to quote monthly, calculating the amount per calendar month, covering discrepancies between lengths of month by multiplying the weekly rent by 52 (for the number of weeks in a year) then dividing by 12 (to get a monthly rent). Most letting agents in central London will quote weekly rates, while in inner London and suburbs, you'll be quoted monthly. But note: just because rents are quoted weekly, this doesn't mean you'll have to pay weekly. The most usual arrangement is to pay calendar monthly by standing order directly to the landlord's bank account.

- *What does the rent include?* You may be quoted exclusive of all bills (the most usual arrangement) or inclusive of all or some bills (most often found in rentals of single rooms in shared houses where divvying up the bills is too much hassle). If your rent is exclusive of bills, you need to budget for electricity, gas, telephone and council tax, plus water. In inclusive arrangements, phone bills are quite often not included. Who is responsible for which bills should be clearly set out in the tenancy agreement (see Tenancy agreements).

Depending on the current state of the market, rents can be negotiable. In a sluggish market, you can make an offer lower than the rent. In a boom market, you may find yourself being gazumped by a rival prepared to pay a higher rent.

Where to look for properties?

Traditionally, there have been two main sources of information on properties to rent: local newspapers, magazines and shopwindows or lettings agents.

Local newspapers, magazines and shop windows

Open any newspaper and you will see column after column of rooms, flats and houses to let. Magazines published in all major cities and magazines for specific sectors of the community – ethnic minorities, gays and lesbians – also have To Let columns. This is how an estimated 50 per cent of all tenants find their properties. It's a dog eat dog world if this is your choice. Demand for decent, reasonably priced rooms and flats within commuting distance of town centres almost always outstrips supply and a familiar sight in most areas is that of would-be tenants buying the latest edition of the local newspaper, turning to the property ads and immediately getting on the mobile or into the nearest phone box. Some landlords operate a first come, first served policy but many more are quite picky.

The tighter your budget, the more likely you are to find potential suitable properties through newspapers or local notices. But remember you're on your own if you use this method. It's up to you to insist on a signed written agreement. Most landlords will want this anyway if they have any sense because they can't go through the county courts accelerated possessions procedure without a written contract. (See Repossessing your property through the courts.) The landlord will ask for a deposit of between a month and six weeks' rent but there's currently nothing to stop him putting it in his own bank account and refusing to hand it back at the end of the tenancy on some spurious ground. You must insist the landlord take an inventory (see later) at the beginning and end of the tenancy so that you can't be unjustly accused of damaging or losing property.

DID YOU KNOW?

Landlords cannot discriminate against you on grounds of:

- colour
- race
- creed
- nationality
- sex
- disability.

But they can and *do* discriminate on grounds of:

- family composition (singles or couples only)
- number and age of children
- pets
- type of employment
- unemployment
- sexuality.

There's also covert discrimination in favour of the respectable looking. Landlords want someone they think will keep the property tidy and not cause the neighbours to complain about loud late night parties. If you want to find somewhere to live, suppress your outlandish tendencies until you've signed the tenancy agreement.

▶

If you're on housing benefit (HB), it will almost certainly take longer to find somewhere to live. Recent research, 'Housing benefit and private landlords', commissioned by the Department of Transport, Local Government and the Regions from Social and Community Planning Research, showed that three-quarters of landlords identified particular types of household or individuals whom they prefer as tenants. Only 1 per cent of these expressly preferred tenants on housing benefit. Of the two-thirds of landlords who identified particular types of tenants they did not want to let to, 26 per cent mentioned tenants on housing benefit. The main reasons for this were problems with administration and bureaucracy (housing benefit is administered by local authorities, many of whom are struggling with complex rules and inefficient technology); tenants getting into arrears with rent and fears that housing benefit tenants may be noisy and damage the property.

Lettings agents

Any high street worthy of the name should have one or more lettings agents. These range from one-man bands in dusty offices with a desk, a phone and a window full of curling postcards carrying hand-written property details, to high profile offices filled with keen young agents and windows full of glossy photographs. Either way, they want to rent you a property because they will earn a commission from the landlord for doing so. Like estate agents who work for sellers (see Chapter 2), letting agents

If you want to find somewhere to live, suppress your outlandish tendencies until you've signed the tenancy agreement work for landlords and earn a commission (normally 10 to 15 per cent of the monthly rent over the term of the tenancy).

But although the agent isn't technically on the tenant's side, it pays him or her to be helpful to you so that you find a property you like and don't hassle the agent and/or the landlord later on. Agents should be able to give you lists of available properties to get an idea of prices and show you round. They'll do some of the legwork for you, weeding out unsuitable places that you might have wasted time going to see if you'd been on your own. They should explain the tenancy agreement to you and advise you to get an inventory carried out. If they are actively managing the property on behalf of the landlord, a common arrangement, they will carry out an inventory for you.

The lettings industry is currently unregulated, just like the sales industry. Your best protection is to choose a firm which is a member of the Association of Residential Letting Agents (ARLA, **www.arla.co.uk**). Currently 1200 firms are members, including every type of agency from national chains to specialist independents. ARLA members have to comply with a code of practice, demonstrate certain levels of training and competence and take out professional indemnity insurance. Most importantly for tenants, they also have to hold money from deposits in separate client accounts so that your funds are protected if the firm collapses. Many agencies that aren't ARLA members have no separate accounts for holding deposits and just use your money as part of their working capital. If they subsequently go out of business, you have little chance of getting your money back as many tenants have discovered to their cost.

A more recent source of information on properties to let is the internet.

The internet

The last few years have seen an explosion of sites advertising properties to
let. As with buying and selling sites, they fall into two categories: those set
up by individual agents and aggregated sites or property portals with
search engines allowing you to look for properties from different agents by
postcode, town or region. The internet is an excellent place to start
searching and get details of properties to rent online. But bear in mind that
there's a very quick turnaround in the rental market and only the most
assiduous agents who update their sites daily can keep up. The internet is
also only a starting point, an electronic shop window which allows you to
contact agents. Once you get to the viewing stage, it's get-on-your-bike
time, targeting the agents with properties in your price range.

WEB WATCH

➡ Most of the major property portals reviewed in Chapters 1 and 2 also feature
properties to rent. Searching for rental property is a similar procedure to searching
for property for sale, with the same provisos – you're limited to the agents who
choose to sign up for particular sites, some of the properties will be gone by the
time you get the details on screen and coverage of some parts of the country is
patchy. As well as the high profile property sites, check out the following.

➡ www.letonthenet.com

Claim: '1000s of properties to rent in London and throughout the UK.' 'The aim
is to provide a seamless online experience.'

How it works: Search for properties by area. Clicking on large areas like
London and other cities brings up a breakdown of areas. You can search for
properties by type and number of bedrooms. There's also a useful list of tips
for tenants, a moving in guide and change of address facility provided by
www.simplymove.co.uk (see Chapter 6). Local London area guides are
provided by **www.thisislondon.co.uk,** the online arm of the London *Evening
Standard*.

Pros: Easy to navigate.

Cons: Choice of property and agents limited – a search for property to rent in one south east London postcode turned up nothing. If the search produces nothing, you have to go back to the beginning of the search process to start a new search.

➡ **www.easylet.org.uk**

➡ Site aimed primarily at landlords, offering insurance for rented property, mortgage quotations for buying to let and downloadable documents including tenancy agreements. A simple, unfussy site with no flashing advertising or other distractions.

➡ **www.lettingweb.com**

➡ Specializes in property to let in Scotland.

The art of viewing

Often when you go into a property for the first time, you can tell immediately whether you can imagine living there. You hate it because it's dark/the bedroom overlooks a backyard with overflowing dustbins/the bathroom reminds you of your old school cloakroom. Or you love it because it's bright/light/on the right floor/has attractive views/a beautiful kitchen.

But before you sign up on the spot for your dream home check:

● *Boilers and heating equipment.* Do gas boilers and solid fuel heaters look old and/or badly maintained? Badly installed or malfunctioning boilers and heaters are a particular danger because they can give off carbon monoxide fumes – colourless, odourless and potentially lethal. A build up of carbon monoxide poisoning can cause nausea, vomiting, chest and stomach pains and long exposure can kill you. Look for a pilot light or flame burning orange instead of blue. Ask to see a gas safety certificate. By law landlords have to have appliances serviced by a

Often when you go into

a property for the first time,

you can tell immediately

whether you can imagine living there

CORGI-registered engineer every 12 months and provide you with a copy of the certificate.

- *Condensation/damp*. Look for flaking paint or uneven, crumpled wallpaper which could signal damp patches. If it starts at floor level in a basement, it could be rising damp. Patches appearing half-way up walls could mean a leak from an outside pipe. Condensation, where bathrooms or kitchens aren't ventilated properly, creates black mould, especially in corners of rooms, up outside walls and around window frames. Such defects aren't, of course, your responsibility to repair but they're a sign of neglect and living in damp conditions is unpleasant and unhealthy.

ACTION POINT ➡

REFERENCES

Before you take possession, you will have to produce the addresses of several references. One of these will be from your bank to confirm that you are 'good for the rent'. Another will be from your previous landlord if you have rented before. Your employer, solicitor and accountant are other potential referees. So be ready with addresses of suitable people. If you go through an ARLA letting agent, you can expect your details to be checked against the Association's database of blacklisted tenants. The database is designed to protect agents and landlords against tenants with a history of trashing property or not paying rents.

The tenancy agreement – what to look for

The assured shorthold tenancy

When you've found the property you want and agreed a rent, you will be asked to sign a tenancy agreement. In England and Wales, this will be an assured shorthold tenancy. This entitles you to live in the property for an initial period, normally six months, paying a market rent. You can agree a fixed term of less than six months if you are looking for a short-term rental. Alternatively, you can set it up as a periodic tenancy, so that the agreement runs on indefinitely from one rental period to the next.

The key things to remember about an assured shorthold tenancy are:

- The landlord can repossess your property automatically at any time after the first six months by giving you two months' notice.

- Even if you've initially agreed a term of less than six months, the landlord doesn't have a guaranteed right to possession until six months are up.

- But he can seek repossession during the first six months if:

  - you are in arrears with your rent

  - you gave false information to secure the tenancy in the first place

  - the landlord is behind with his mortgage payments, the lender wants to repossess the property and the tenancy agreement made it clear from the outset that this could constitute grounds for repossession.

Assured tenancy

This is much rarer than an assured shorthold tenancy, thanks to changes in the Housing Act of 1996. This declared that all new tenancies after February 28 1997 would automatically be assured shortholds, unless landlords deliberately followed a special procedure to set up an assured tenancy. The main difference between an assured tenancy and an assured shorthold is that with the former, the landlord doesn't have an automatic right to repossess the property after an initial period. This is obviously good news for tenants wanting security of tenure but not so good for landlords. If you're already renting on an assured tenancy, your landlord can't replace it with a shorthold agreement at the end of the term.

ACTION POINT ➡

The Department of Transport, Local Government and the Regions, formerly the Department of Environment, Transport and the Regions, has a number of clearly written and informative leaflets for Landlords and Tenants available online at **www.dtlr.gov.uk**.

Fees and deposits

Fees

As a tenant, you shouldn't have to pay a fee to an agency to find you a property. Agents are paid by the landlord. But you may have to pay an administration fee to cover the agent's time for taking the inventory (see later), chasing up references and preparing the tenancy agreement. The more upmarket the letting agent the more expensive it will be. Hamptons International, which is active in the more expensive parts of London and the south east, quotes typical costs of £80 for administration, £80 for inventory check in/check out and a referencing fee of £20 per tenant.

Deposits

All landlords, unless they're absurdly trusting, will ask for a deposit and a month's rent in advance. The deposit can be anything from a month's to six weeks' rent. The deposit is to cover damage to the property during your tenure (but not wear and tear which are considered to be part of normal rental expenses, which landlords can set against tax; see later).

Fair enough. But the big problem for many people is getting the deposit back at the end of their tenancy, particularly if the deposit is being held by a landlord rather than an agent as stakeholder. The National Association of Citizens' Advice Bureaux (NACAB, **www.nacab.org.uk**) has been campaigning for years for the establishment of a national disputes resolution mechanism which would adjudicate on deposit disputes and pay out quickly. NACAB published a disturbing report in 1998 which revealed that nearly half of all tenants who had been private tenants in the past five years who were questioned by CABx around the country had had their deposits 'unreasonably withheld' and only one in six of these had managed to get their money back. Case studies in the report suggested a pattern of widespread abuse of tenants by landlords, who withheld deposits with little or no justification. Currently, the only redress available to tenants is to take landlords to the small claims court. Not only can it take months to get a hearing, but even if the tenant wins, it's up to him or her actually to enforce the judgment, by an attachment of earnings order or sending in the bailiffs.

The good news for tenants is that a scheme to safeguard rental deposits is finally being piloted and is being supported by ARLA. Under the scheme, landlords and tenants in dispute over the return of deposits will be able to take their cases to the independent housing ombudsman (**www.ihos.org.uk**) who will adjudicate within 10 working days. The scheme will be free to tenants, while landlords will have to pay £20 if the ombudsman finds in favour of the tenants. Once the ombudsman has decided the case, the deposit will be paid back to the winning party by an insurance company which guarantees payouts under the scheme.

Inventories – how they protect you

One of the simplest and most effective ways of protecting yourself against arguments over damage to the property is to insist that an inventory is taken at the beginning of the tenancy and again at the end. The inventory is a list of everything in the property that isn't yours. It should include details of:

- carpets

- curtains

- décor

- kitchen and bathroom fittings

- the contents of all kitchen cupboards/drawers not belonging to you

- any bedding/soft furnishings

- all furniture belonging to the landlord.

As well as listing the contents, the inventory should describe the appearance and condition of each item at the beginning of the tenancy. This detailed information must be signed by landlord and tenant. If there's any dispute over the condition of the property, the inventory should provide the necessary evidence.

If you have found your property through a letting agent, the agent will probably do the inventory at the beginning and end of your tenancy, and will hold your deposit on behalf of the landlord. But the agent can't return your deposit without the agreement of the landlord.

As well as listing the contents, the inventory should describe the appearance and condition of each item at the beginning of the tenancy

Your rights during your tenancy

- You have a right to live in a rented property as if it is your home. The landlord has to ask your permission before coming into the property.

- The landlord has a right to inspect the property or carry out repairs 'at reasonable times of day' but must give you 24 hours' notice in writing and stick to any conditions set out in the tenancy agreement.

- You can't be evicted without a possession order from a court.

Your obligations during your tenancy

- You must pay the rent on time and in the way agreed.

- You must take care of the property and use it responsibly. Holding wild parties will mean complaints from the neighbours and could be grounds for eviction, as could using it for 'illegal or immoral' purposes.

- You must keep to the terms of the tenancy agreement. For example, if the agreement excludes the keeping of pets, you could be evicted if you yield to the temptation to feed the stray cat hanging around.

- You must pay bills for which you're responsible, as set out in the agreement. (See Rents: What to look for, earlier.)

Landlords

Preparing your property to let

In a market where demand almost always outstrips supply, you will usually be able to find someone desperate enough to rent even the shoddiest, dirtiest hole. But don't expect to get good tenants, keep it fully let or bring in an income which makes being a landlord worthwhile.

173

Assuming you don't want to make a living as a latter day Peter Rachman, you will probably either be letting out your own property or letting one that you have bought for the purpose. Buy to let properties are dealt with in detail in the next section.

Letting your own home

Before you put your own property on the market to let, check that:

- all appliances have been serviced and work properly

- anything that is broken has been mended

- you haven't left anything that is irreplaceable or of sentimental value if you're letting it furnished (but this doesn't mean stripping the house of everything that makes it a home)

- if you're letting the property furnished, you remove any furniture which doesn't comply with fire regulations (see later)

- you inform your mortgage lender, and your freeholder if your property is leasehold. Mortgage lenders reserve the right to charge a higher rate of interest if you let the property, on the ground that you've changed the terms of your mortgage agreement and introduced a commercial risk.

Is it worth employing an agent?

Or to put it another way, do you want to pay 10 per cent of your rental income in commission to someone to find you a tenant? The answer is probably yes, unless you want to spend hours showing people round your home, drawing up tenancy agreements and chasing up references. Especially if you're letting your own home (because you've been relocated elsewhere temporarily for example), you will want to have tenants thoroughly checked out.

Use an agent who is a member of the Association of Residential Letting Agents (ARLA) (see Letting agents earlier in this chapter). This isn't a guarantee of impeccable service and efficiency but it's as close as you're going to get in an industry which still harbours more than its fair share of cowboys.

Decide whether you want the agent just to find you a tenant and draw up the relevant tenancy agreement or whether you want your property managed by the agent during the tenancy as well. The latter approach has pros and cons.

Pros

- You won't have to deal with awful late night calls from tenants saying the boiler isn't working and demanding immediate service. Letting agents have their own contractors and won't let themselves be forced into finding an emergency heating engineer from the Yellow Pages.

- Letting agents visit regularly to check on the property, which is reassuring especially if you're a long way away.

- Letting agents will do the incoming and outgoing inventories for you as part of the service, providing a second pair of critical eyes if there is a dispute over damage.

Cons

- It costs more, usually around 15 per cent of your rental income, compared with around 10 per cent for a tenant's introductory service.

- Some agents work harder for this fee than others.

- You may find yourself checking up on the agent as much as the tenants.

~~Safety~~ ~~Re~~gulations

Landlords used to be able to let out properties full of boilers with
blocked vents, furniture filled with highly flammable foam and electric
cables fraying. But the rules have been tightened up considerably over
the past few years and you risk swingeing fines and even a prison
sentence if you ignore the rules and a tenant in your property is injured
or killed through your negligence.

You must:

- make sure that all gas appliances including cookers, water heaters,
  fires and boilers plus flues serving these appliances, are serviced every
  12 months by a CORGI-registered gas installer. You have to provide
  the tenant with a copy of the gas safety certificate showing the checks
  have been carried out.

- check that electric wiring and appliances are safe, and provide
  instruction booklets where relevant. There are no set testing intervals
  as there are with gas appliances, but you are expected to have electrics
  checked by a qualified engineer and keep records of the checks.

- ensure that furniture and fittings, including sofas, beds and other
  upholstered furnishings comply with resistance requirements under
  the Furniture and Fittings (Fire) (Safety) Regulations 1988. All new

You risk swingeing fines and

even a prison sentence

if you ignore the rules and

a tenant in your property ## is injured or killed

through your negligence

and secondhand furniture must comply (there should be a label on each item confirming that it does) unless it was made before 1950. If you replace furniture in properties you're already letting, this too must comply. If you can show you're just letting the property on a one-off temporary basis, you're exempt from these rules (it would obviously be absurd to force people to replace all the furniture in their home if they were just moving abroad to work for a year) but as soon as it becomes a business and you let your property to a series of tenants, through an agent, you will be subject to the regulations.

How easy is it to get your property back?

Easier than it used to be but not as easy as many landlords would like. Tenants fall into three main categories, in ascending order of ease of eviction.

Sitting tenants

Also called statutory or protected tenants. Very few new sitting tenancies have been created since 1989 but there are still a number of mostly elderly people who have occupied the same property for years, paying minimal rents and living as tenants under the rules of the 1977 Rent Act. As long as they continue to stay there, they can't be evicted and they can't be forced to pay a market rent. Instead, their rents are reviewed regularly by a rent assessment committee. The only way you will normally come across these people is if you buy the freehold of a property at auction which includes one or more sitting tenants in the package. Such properties can be a bargain for a buy to let investment, especially if they meet other criteria for choosing a good buy to let property (see later). But you risk having one or more units in your property unprofitably occupied, perhaps for years. Cruel though it seems, the best sitting tenant buys are when the tenant is aged 80 or over. A husband or wife living in the property has the right to inherit a statutory tenancy after the death of a partner. Others who have lived in the property with a statutory tenant for at least two years can continue living in the property but on an assured tenancy.

Assured tenancies

These allow you to charge a market rent but give the tenant better security. If you want to repossess a property let on an assured tenancy you have to show the court that you have good reason for doing so. Before the end of February 1997, tenancies agreed under the terms of the Housing Act 1988 (see earlier section, The tenancy agreement – what to look for) were set up as assured tenancies. Landlords wanting to ensure they could get their property back after the first six months without having to go through the administrative hassle of serving a notice to that effect at the beginning of the tenancy had to specify an assured shorthold agreement.

Assured shorthold tenancies

These allow you to charge a market rent and automatically get your property back after six months. New tenancies started after 28 February 1997 are set up as shortholds unless you specifically say otherwise.

Getting your property back

What happens if you've served all the right notices, your tenants are on an assured shorthold tenancy with all the right paperwork, the day comes for them to vacate the property…and they don't leave?

Don't:

- be tempted to try and evict them yourself
- send round a group of your largest and most threatening friends to do the job for you
- bar the door and prevent the tenants from entering the property.

Any of these could lead to a damages action by the tenants which they would probably win. You have to have a court order to evict tenants.

Repossessing your property through the courts

There are a number of grounds for possession. Some of these are mandatory, meaning that as long as the paperwork is correct, you will get a possession order under the accelerated possession procedure, which should take three to six weeks. Some mandatory grounds need prior notice – you must have served notice at the beginning of the tenancy that you may serve notice on this ground. Others are discretionary, which means the courts may or may not grant a possession order.

These are some of the mandatory grounds for possession:

- You used to live in the property as your home and you want to do so again (prior notice needed).

- You're in arrears with a mortgage granted on the property before it was let out and your lender wants to repossess it (prior notice needed).

- You want to redevelop the property and can't do it with the tenant living there.

- Your tenant owes at least two months' rent if he pays monthly or eight weeks' rent if he pays weekly.

You may be able to claim possession on discretionary grounds if the tenant:

- was behind with the rent when you served notice of repossession and when you started court proceedings

- has broken any other term of the tenancy agreement

- has trashed the property or allowed someone else to do so

- has damaged the furniture

- obtained the tenancy in the first place under false pretences.

If the tenant still won't go after you've obtained a court order, you must ask the court to appoint a bailiff.

Buy to let

Buying property to let out started to catch on seriously among investors in the 1990s, as astute buyers moved in to hoover up cheap properties during the recession and let them out to take advantage of the more flexible types of tenancies introduced in the 1988 Housing Act. Mortgage lenders, which had previously charged higher rates to property investors claiming that such investments constituted commercial lending, relaxed their stance and introduced competitive rates. A group of major lenders including the Alliance & Leicester, Clydesdale Bank, Halifax Mortgage Services, Mortgage Express, NatWest Mortgage Services and Paragon Mortgages, banded together with ARLA and formally launched the Buy to Let scheme, to encourage private individuals to invest in rental property.

Choosing the right property

As the property market picked itself off the floor in the mid-1990s, buying property to rent started to look like an increasingly lucrative investment. Prices were rising so the capital value of a property investment rose. There was a healthy demand for rental property as the working population became more affluent and more mobile, with the growth of contract working. The words 'smart property' and 'rent' were no longer a contradiction in terms.

But buying a property to let doesn't just mean popping into the nearest estate agent and picking up something you wouldn't mind living in yourself. Investment property requires an understanding of local rental markets and what tenants are looking for in your chosen area. As many would-be landlords have discovered, getting this wrong means months where property is empty or having to accept a lower rent than you need to cover expenses and still make a profit. This may not be a total disaster if the capital value of your property is still rising, but many people decided to take their profit and sell rather than continue to try letting the wrong type of property.

ARLA DOS AND DON'TS OF BUYING TO LET

Do:

- think of buying as a medium to long-term investment.

- check out local market conditions with an ARLA agent.

- work out your sums. Will your rent cover your mortgage plus costs (such as repairs, maintenance and service charges) even if you have a couple of void periods, where the property is empty for a month or more?

- decorate and fit out the property to a high standard especially kitchens and bathrooms. Neutral colours are best. Clean, well decorated properties let quickly.

- use an ARLA agent.

Don't:

- buy something just because you like it. It may not be suitable for letting. The key question to ask is: What type of properties are in demand? Is the area full of students looking for shared houses? Or are they families who have relocated for a couple of years? Or is there big demand for two-bedroom flats for professionals? Are most tenants commuters who need to be near a station? Agents estimate that anything more than 10 minutes' walk from a station will be more difficult to let.

- buy something with a lot of potential maintenance problems like a large garden or an old period house needing a lot of upkeep.

- rely on do-it-yourself documentation. Get a specialist agent to draw up the tenancy agreement, inventories and make sure the right notices are served at the right time.

- use secondhand furniture or fittings which could contravene fire and furnishing regulations.

WEB WATCH

➡ The following websites have useful information for potential buy to let investors. **www.arla.co.uk** includes a complete list of ARLA members. For more information on buy to let and how it works, go to **www.buytolet.co.uk**. For the latest on buy to let mortgages, go to **www.buytolet.co.uk/mortgages**.

Your investment priorities

You obviously want to make money from buying property to let, otherwise you wouldn't do it. But what sort of money? Are you more interested in seeing the capital investment in your property grow? Or do you want to generate lots of income? Or both?

Thanks to sharply rising prices in some parts of the UK over the past couple of years, some investors, especially those who bought as prices started to rise again after the recession, have seen both the value of their properties rise and a good rental yield.

But generally speaking, if you buy in a more expensive area, you will pay more for your property in the first place. When you add in borrowings and costs, your return will be lower than on a property which is cheaper to buy in the first place.

Figure 7.1   Property investment calculator

PROPERTY INVESTMENT CALCULATOR

This calculator has been designed to assist you in appraising a potential residential property investment.
We strongly recommend that you contact your nearest ARLA agent to help with completing this form. They will also be able to help assess demand, likly rental values, and void periods.
For help on mortgages for Buy to Let look at the Buy to Let website.

Website assistance:

ARLA members can be found at   www.arla.co.uk
Buy to Let - how it works   www.buytolet.co.uk
The latest mortgage information at   www.buytolet.co.uk/mortgages

PROPERTY PURCHASE	
Purchase Price	
Legal Costs	
Stamp Duty	
Survey Fee	
TOTAL PURCHASE	A

NETT RETURN BEFORE TAX	
TOTAL RENTAL	B
TOTAL COSTS	C
NETT RETURN BEFORE TAX (B-C)	D
Percentage Return	

INCOME	
Rental per month/week	
Annual Rental	
Void periods allowance(eg. 1 month P.A.)	
TOTAL RENTAL	B

WITH BORROWING	
NETT RETURN	D
ANNUAL MORTGAGE REPAYMENTS	E
AMOUNT OF CAPITAL (i.e. DEPOSIT) PUT DOWN FOR PURCHASE	F
NETT RETURN BEFORE TAX ON YOUR CASH INVESTMENT D-E x100/F	

EXPENSES	
Letting and Management fees (Inc. VAT)	
Rent Insurance Inc. IPT	
Ground Rent (if any)	
Service Charge/Building Insurance	
Repairs/Maintanance	
Gas/Heating Service Contract	
Safety Cerfficates Gas/Electricity etc.	
TOTAL COSTS	C

Example:

Assume the return at D is £5,000 and your capital/deposit at F is £12,000 and the mortgage repayments are £3000

Then: £5,000 - £3,000 = £2,000 x 100 = £200,000 divided by £12,000 = 16.6%

CAPITAL VALUES

To check the movement in capital values, there are various property market indices available on websites and published in the press.

TAXATION

Net rental income is subject to income tax at the marginal rate, but all expenses of a revenue nature are allowable, including loan interest. Furthermore, a wear and tear allowance of 10% of the rent, less water rates, is available where the property is furnished.

Capital gains on investment property are subject to Capital Gains Tax, also at the marginal rate, and will vary according to the length of time property in held.

Source: Association of Residential Letting Agents (ARLA)

Tax matters

Your net rental income (in other words your income after costs like mortgage payments and repairs) is taxable at your highest marginal rate. But there are generous rules for allowable expenses including wear and tear at 10 per cent of the rent for furnished properties. You can also set the whole of the cost of mortgage borrowing against tax, which makes it worth being highly geared as long as you're confident you can keep your property tightly rented.

Because your investment property isn't your main residence, you will also have to pay capital gains tax when you sell, again at your highest marginal rate.

You will have to declare income and capital gains on your annual tax return, remembering to ask the Inland Revenue for the relevant property pages.

8

OFF THE WALL
WAYS TO BUY
SELL AND RENT

BY THE END OF THIS CHAPTER YOU WILL

· ·

- ● Wonder why we don't all just swap homes over the internet

· ·

- ● Know if you have the nerve to buy or sell at auction

· ·

- ● Understand the true meaning of 'property porn', as you surreptitiously log on at work to overseas property sites for longing glances at luxury villas in the south of France

· ·

There are times when the prospect of buying and selling property in the usual way (go to estate agent, put property on market, find buyer, sell it) are too slow, too unpredictable or just plain impossible. Try selling a property which hasn't been updated for 30 years complete with sitting tenant through a high street estate agent rather than at auction.

Think of this chapter as the 'and finally' of this guide. This is where you'll find out how to take advantage of more unorthodox (but of course still legal) methods of getting the property you want. And if you're one of the growing band of UK nationals who have realized that a property overseas can be (a) cheaper, (b) easier to get to and (c) a lot closer to delicious food and wine and sunny weather than anything this side of the channel, you'll find tips on how to buy and details on some of the best websites here too.

Take advantage of the more unorthodox methods of getting the property you want

But, first, how to get what you want, when you want, how you want in the UK without having to go through the pain of a chain or wait six months to seal a deal only to have the other side drop out at the last minute.

House swapping

This is a wonderfully efficient way to buy a property. You find a property you want and the owner of your dream home wants yours too. So you swap. There's no chain because you're buying each others' homes rather than selling your home to one person and buying from someone completely different. Both sides in a homeswap have a massive incentive to go through with the transaction because they desperately want each others' properties.

The biggest difficulty is finding someone to swap with, who wants to sell at the same time as you want to buy, who has a property you want and who wants yours as well. Most swaps occur because one side is trading down, following a divorce or children leaving home for example, while the other side is trading up.

In theory, your estate agent should be the key player in any swap arrangement. Agents have large numbers of people on their books who are registered with them and who have provided details of their requirements. They should know someone who has the four-bedroom family home you covet and who would like nothing more than your trendy loft apartment which you can no longer live in because the children keep falling down the spiral staircase from the mezzanine.

But this sort of 'joined-up' estate agency appears to be beyond all but a few enterprising agents. So it's up to you to ask if there are any likely swappees on your agent's books.

In practice, most swaps happen through pure coincidence, often when potential buyers come to look round your property, say they love it but have something to sell and that something just happens to be the very thing you're looking for.

Save money by swapping

Unless you're an avid reader of Inland Revenue press releases or obscure pages on the Revenue's excellent website at **www.inlandrevenue.gov.uk**, you probably don't know that you can save massive amounts of money by

You can save massive amounts of money by swapping your home,

if you're the one trading down

swapping your home, if you're the one trading down. Say you have a house worth £300,000 and you want to swap it for a flat worth £200,000. The owner of the flat will be paying for your house partly in cash and partly in kind, with the flat. As far as the Revenue is concerned, this is not a sale, on which you would have to pay stamp duty (of £2000 at 1 per cent of the selling price), but a transfer, on which you have to pay a notional sum of just £5. But to make sure you don't end up paying full stamp duty by accident, solicitors must draw up the deal as a single contract with the more expensive property paid for partly in kind and partly in cash. Swapping properties worth very similar prices also won't work because you must exchange more than a nominal sum in cash to be eligible for the saving.

You may save on estate agents' fees as long as you genuinely find your swap match independently (online or through personal contacts). But if you originally put your property on with an agent, which can argue that it introduced your swapper, or you were brought together through an estate agent, you will have to pay commission.

WEB WATCH

➡ www.webswappers.com

Claim: More than 750 properties for swap listed on its site, with more than 150 flats and 480 houses at the last count.

How it works: You can swap anything from CDs to TVs but property swaps are growing in popularity, says website director Jonathan Attwood. You can register on the site for free. Click on the list of properties for swap to get more information. If you find something you like, you can email the owner directly. House swapping is popular with council flat tenants who don't want to get trapped in the mire of council housing department bureaucracy but there are plenty of owner occupiers wanting to skip chains and meet up with a like-minded homeowner.

Pros: Easy to use and it gets results – so far around a dozen people have actually achieved swaps, and up to 40 people have requested one of the site's To Swap boards – a bit more attention grabbing than a For Sale board, says Attwood.

Cons: Success still depends on finding the right fellow swapper at the right time.

Auctions

Buying

Buying at auction is a nervewracking prospect for most people who have never done it. What if you blow your nose and discover you have bought a three-bedroom terrace in Croydon or a two up, two down in Oldham? What if you get carried away with the bidding and discover you've committed yourself to more money than you can come up with?

Auctioneers will reassure you that your first fear should be unfounded, as any experienced practitioner should be able to tell the difference between a serious bidder and someone who's just reaching for their handkerchief. But fear number two is very real, because once you make the highest bid for a property at auction, it's yours and you have to come up with the cash. As Countrywide Property Auctions, one of the UK's biggest auctioneers, warns prospective buyers: 'At the drop of the gavel in the auction room, the property is yours, contracts are considered exchanged and it is too late to cancel the sale if you come across a problem.'

191

Buying at auction is a nervewracking prospect for most people who have never done it

This immediate commitment is the key difference between buying on the open market and buying at auction. Here are the important things to remember if you're thinking about buying at auction:

- One of the big attractions of auctions is that they cut out the horrible weeks of waiting and to-ing and fro-ing between making an offer and exchanging contracts inherent in the traditional housebuying system (see Chapter 3). The auction is the equivalent of exchanging contracts and you're expected to have checked out the property and organized the money in the period between the publication of the catalogue giving details of properties and the auction itself (normally four weeks).

- But don't think you're safe from gazumpers at auction. It just happens more quickly. You can easily find yourself outbid, having spent money on surveyors, solicitors and a legal pack for the property. This is a chance you have to take.

- Put yourself on the mailing lists of as many firms of auctioneers as you can. (See Web Watch.) When you get the catalogues and see properties you like, contact the agent as soon as possible for a viewing.

- Viewing a property for sale at auction is the same as viewing any other property. Remember the basics: don't be overwhelmed by the awfulness/beauty of the interior décor – you can change this easily. Most important, how structurally sound is the property? Has it got dry rot/damp/infestations? When was it replumbed/rewired/reroofed?

Such structural repairs can cost a lot and are often likely to be necessary on properties put into auction because they'd be tricky to sell on the normal open market. A full structural survey (see Chapter 3) is a good investment. Alright, so you might be outbid on the day, in which case you'll have spent money for nothing but if you get the property, you'll have invaluable advice on the condition and value for money the property represents. And if you've got any sense, you'd pay for a full structural survey or at least a homebuyer's report if you were buying in the normal way and you'd be no more certain at the surveying/valuation stage that you'd actually get the property.

- Get an idea of how well valued the property is by talking to local agents and your surveyor and compare it with similar properties in agents' windows and on the internet (see Chapter 1).

- Ask a solicitor to examine the contents of any legal packs provided by the auctioneers. Countrywide, for example, provides a £15 pack which includes the special conditions of sale, local searches, Land Registry office copies and copies of leases.

- You will need a deposit (normally of 10 per cent unless the property is very cheap or sold at a knockdown price), which you must pay at the auction by cash, building society cheque or banker's draft (some auctioneers will accept personal cheques with ID). And by the time you get to the auction, you must be in a position to pay the balance of the price either in cash or with a mortgage with a firm mortgage offer. If you don't come up with the balance 20 working days from the date of the contract exchanged on auction day, you face severe penalties.

Selling

Selling at auction can be an excellent way of shifting your property quickly, especially if it's frankly a bit of a dump or there are legal problems which would be costly to put right and which are putting off mainstream buyers. It can also net you a better price than on the open market, as potential buyers compete against each other for your property. Auctions attract investors and developers who are keen to hoover up properties – although don't expect these characters to pay top whack. They're in this strictly for the money and their value to you is in getting properties off your hands.

Consider selling at auction if:

- the property is tenanted, especially if there's a sitting tenant who looks set to stay sitting for the foreseeable future (see Chapter 7). If there are tenants on assured shorthold tenancies, where the landlord can automatically get the property back after the first six months on serving the right notices, you may find an investor on the open market happy to take it off your hands with the tenant in situ. If the tenant pays the rent on time and is generally well behaved, he or she is worth a lot to an investor, saving the time and effort of finding a new tenant.

- you own the freehold of a property split up into flats sold off on long leases. Freeholds are usually sold at auction, although remember that you must legally offer the freehold to the leaseholders to buy jointly before selling it on. The value of a freehold depends partly on the amount of ground rent it produces over the term of the lease and partly on how long the leases have got left to run before they fall in and the property reverts to the freeholder.

- you own a property with a defective lease which would cost you a lot to put right. There's no such thing as a standard lease (see Chapter 3) and some leases were drawn up with clauses which have subsequently proved unworkable, out of date or unacceptable to most buyers and their solicitors. For example, most leaseholders wouldn't now want a lease which allowed the landlord to claw back his legal costs from a leaseholder dispute out of the service charges paid by those same leaseholders. But some leases are still drafted like this and the landlord would have to agree to any amendment. Other leases don't provide properly for the building to be insured as a whole. Similarly, out-of-date leases have been known to say there's no access to the garden for certain flats when this has changed, or to say there's a single shared central heating boiler when all flats have since had individual boilers installed but no one's bothered to change the lease.

- you own property but the land on which it stands is more of an attraction for developers than the property.

- your property is derelict or damaged in some way. A good proportion of any properties at auction are boarded up and not accessible to prospective buyers, which puts off most buyers on the open market. Buyers at auction are less picky – although don't expect big prices.

WEB WATCH

➡ You can already bid for property at auction over the telephone and the logical next steps are to be able to bid over the internet. Large auctioneers include Countrywide (**www.eigroup.co.uk**), Allsops (**www.allsop.co.uk**), Winkworth (for London) (**www.winkworth.co.uk**) and Barnard Marcus (**www.auctions.co.uk/property/barnard.htm**).

➡ If you don't fancy the cut and thrust of the auction room and prefer to bid over the internet, go to:

➡ www.propwatch.com

Background: Started by a group of 'Londoners, for Londoners as a low cost alternative to the traditional estate agent'.

Claim: 'Do you want to buy or sell your home for the best possible price without an estate agent?'

How it works: This innovative site allows you to buy and sell properties at auction. Registration is free. You search for properties by area, choosing from the counties of England and Wales, London, Birmingham, Manchester,

Newcastle and Bristol. Clicking on London, for example, gives you a map of London boroughs, which in turns breaks down into a comprehensive list of areas showing how many properties are being auctioned in each area. Property details include useful features like what bids have already been submitted, what the highest bid is so far and how much longer the auction has to run, in days, hours and minutes. Icons indicate which properties have seen the most active bidding and which are still on the market. The key difference between this and a physical auction is that your bid isn't immediately binding but subject to contract like an open sale. No money changes hands when your bid is accepted. Instead you carry out all the searches and so on, then exchange contracts. So why bother? Propwatch claims that it allows you to cut out estate agents and stimulate a bidding process which should bring you a higher end price. A mortgage calculator helps you work out how much you can afford.

Verdict: Bidding process translates well to the net. Site easy to navigate.

Buying overseas

If buying at auction is nervewracking, think how much worse it could be trying to buy a property in a foreign language when you're unfamiliar with the housebuying system and the main aim of the people you're dealing with seems to be to relieve you of large sums in commission.

But none of this stops more and more British people heading across the sea, with France, Spain, Italy, Portugal and the USA the most popular destinations. If the pound is strong, it makes property look cheap. New train routes including the TGV (train à grande vitesse) to Marseilles and new air routes from regional airports in the UK mean that heading to the sun doesn't take any longer than getting to the west country.

Thousands of Britons have successfully bought property abroad so the difficulties are by no means insurmountable. But be careful before you

If buying at auction is **nervewracking, think how much worse** it could be trying to buy a property in a foreign language when you're unfamiliar with the housebuying system

sign anything. All countries have different housebuying systems both from one another and from England and Scotland. The most significant difference between popular overseas buying destinations and England and Wales is that overseas both sides are committed to the sale much earlier in the process and binding contracts are signed subject to conditions such as satisfactory surveys and financial arrangements.

General tips for buying property abroad

- *Buy through a qualified and licensed agent.* In most countries including France, Italy, Spain, Portugal and the USA, agents legally have to be licensed and using an unlicensed agent means there's no comeback if things go wrong.

- *Don't sign anything until you're sure you understand it.* If the estate agent produces a contract out of his drawer and you sign, you'll be committed to buying a property you might not even want on pain of forfeiting a large deposit. Note that estate agents do more of the legal work in countries like the USA and France, and hence charge more commission.

- *Always hire a solicitor (English speaking if you're not fluent in the local language) to act for you.* In some countries, Spain for example, locals often don't use solicitors but you must insist. Your solicitor will check the seller owns the property, that there are no debts attaching to it (you could find yourself becoming liable for your seller's debts if you're not careful) and that planning regulations have been met. Local searches are not as regulated as they are in the UK and it's often a matter of having a quiet chat at the town hall with people who will know whether you have to cross someone's land to get at your water supply or if your house was built without planning permission.

- *Understand the role played by the state notary (notaire in France, notaio in Italy, notario in Spain).* He is a state official, whose only role is to see that the sale is legally completed. He doesn't act for you or the seller.

WEB WATCH

➡ As with other sorts of property buying, the explosion of internet sites advertising overseas properties for sale or rent means you can do some preliminary research and get a good idea of what things are selling for before you start looking round possible properties. Surfing the net and downloading property details complete with colour pictures gives you a host of useful agents' contact names as well as showing you what's on the market.

➡ You'll be on strong ground if you have some idea of what you can get for your money in your chosen area. A number of UK agents have offices and/or associates in countries popular with British buyers. These include Hamptons International (**www.hamptons.co.uk**), Knight Frank (**www.knightfrank.com**) and FPD Savills (**www.fpdsavills.co.uk**).

➡ The following are also worth checking out:

➡**www.french-property-news.com**

Background: The online arm of the magazine *French Property News*.

Claim: 'Properties in all regions of France. Look no further. The most comprehensive list of properties on the internet.'

How it works: You can search by *département* or on a map of French regions for property lists although there's no obvious search engine for inputting individual requirements like numbers of rooms or types of property. Each property has a reference number through which you access full property details and pictures. Other useful features include links to a number of UK-based agents specializing in foreign property, links to services including architects, builders and financial services, an online bookshop and legal tips for buying property in France.

Pros: Easy to use and up to date.

Cons: Flashing ads are distracting.

Verdict: Useful and well supported by agents.

➡ **www.french-property.com**

Claim: 'The world's no. 1 internet site for French property.'

How it works: You search for property specifying region, price range and limiting the results to properties posted recently. Photos are good, with interior as well as exterior shots from several different angles. There's a list of agents advertising on the site, with links to their own sites and an active discussion forum which raises topics like 'Who pays the agent's commission?' and 'Is it easy to get a survey done?'

Verdict: Fun site, easy to use, recommended.

➡ **www.europropertynet.com**

Claim: 'A European-wide real estate service.'

How it works: Carries property from a wide range of countries including France, Spain, Italy, Portugal and Greece, all accessed by clicking on the flag of the relevant nation. A good site to start with if you haven't yet decided where to buy and want some comparables. You can search for properties by

199

region or price and property details are comprehensive, with numbers of rooms, size of plot and special features.

Pros: Wide range of properties in different countries.

Cons: Layout of property lists is confusing, making it difficult to work out which figure is the price. (Prices are in pounds.) Properties are dated from when they're first posted and some of them have been around for a long time.

Verdict: Potentially useful.

➡ For property in Spain, try **www.spanishpropertyco.com**, which specializes in retirement property. Rather wordy pages which take a lot of time (and money) to read but sensible advice about how to buy. For general tips on buying in Spain, go to **www.cornishco.com** a firm of UK lawyers specializing in Spanish property.

GLOSSARY

Aggregated site   Industry term for website carrying property details from a number of different agents. Also known as a property 'portal'.

Arrangement fee   Sum payable to secure a **fixed rate**, **capped rate** or **discount** mortgage offer.

Asking price   The price set by the seller and his agent for a property. It's common for **offers** to be above the asking price in rising markets and below the asking price in falling markets.

Assured shorthold tenancy   Now the usual form of tenancy agreement, whereby a landlord can automatically get the property back after six months if the right notices are served.

Assured tenancy   Less common form of tenancy whereby the landlord doesn't have the automatic right to repossess after six months.

Bargain (Scotland)   When an offer on a property has been accepted. The bargain is made at the **conclusion of missives**.

Best and final offers   Requested by agents when several buyers are competing for a single property. Bids are made in writing to the agent by a set deadline and the seller chooses which bid to accept.

Bridging loan   Loan advanced when a homeowner has bought a new property but not yet sold his or her current home. Loans advanced when contracts have been **exchanged** and both sides are committed are called 'closed'. When contracts haven't been exchanged and there's no commitment, loans are 'open'.

Buyer's market   When the market is falling, sellers are desperate to offload property and will take low prices.

Buy to let   Scheme operated by selected mortgage lenders and the Association of Residential Letting Agents to encourage investors into buying property to let out.

Capped rate   Mortgage rate which can only rise up to a set ceiling or cap for a set number of years but which falls if base rates fall.

Cashback   Cash sum paid to borrowers by lenders as part of certain mortgage deals as incentive.

CAT mark   Mortgage or investment with special conditions including typically low **arrangement fees** and **redemption penalties**. Introduced by the government in a bid to improve mortgage conditions for consumers.

Certificate of lawful development   Certificate issued by local planning authority confirming that an extension or alteration does not need planning permission.

Chain   A series of transactions depending on each other to go through, as sellers need to sell their property in order to buy another. Buyers and sellers caught up in a chain normally have to **exchange contracts** on the same day to ensure everyone is committed.

Collective enfranchisement   The process of clubbing together with other leaseholders in a block of **leasehold** flats and buying the **freehold** of the block. The freehold is normally purchased through a limited company formed by flatowners for the purpose.

Commonhold   A new form of tenure for flats which would allow flatowners to own their homes outright and become members of a commonhold association responsible for the **common parts**.

Common parts   The parts of a shared block that are communally used and maintained, for example, stairs, landings and hallways.

Comparable   A price that has recently been achieved for similar property. Used by agents and surveyors as a guide to **valuing** properties.

Completion date   The date when the property changes hands, the balance of the purchase price is paid over and the keys are given to the new owner.

Conclusion of missives (Scotland)   The point at which the property sale becomes binding and a **bargain** is made.

Conveyancing The legal process of transferring ownership of land and property from one individual or company to another.

Date of entry (Scotland) The point at which the sale of a property is completed.

Deposit Sum payable at **exchange of contracts**. Usually between 5 per cent and 10 per cent although exact amount is negotiable.

Discount Mortgage rate reduced by set number of percentage points for a specified time.

Downvaluing The **valuation** put on a property by the lender's surveyor is lower than the price the buyer is prepared to pay.

Draft contract Early version of contract drawn up by seller's solicitor including the names and addresses of both parties, the price paid for the property and a **completion date**.

Drive-by Slang term for **valuations** where the valuer merely drives by to check the property exists, without going inside.

Endowment Savings/insurance policy often linked to an interest-only mortgage to build up money to pay off the loan at the end.

Exchange of contracts The stage in the housebuying process in England and Wales at which a deal becomes binding.

First refusal The legal right of flatowners in leasehold flats to be offered the freehold of their block first if the freeholder wants to sell.

Fixed rate A mortgage rate that is fixed for a set period, usually two, three or five years.

Flexible mortgage A loan which allows over- or underpayment and which can be set against a current account to reduce the overall outstanding debt.

Freehold Outright ownership of a property and the land on which it stands. Most houses are owned freehold. In buildings divided into flats, the building itself (the structure and the **common parts**) are owned by a freeholder, while the flats within the building are **leasehold**.

Gazumping   A seller accepts a firm offer for his property, then drops the buyer in favour of another offering a higher price in a rising market. Legal at any time between **offer** and **exchange of contracts**.

Gazundering   A buyer makes a firm offer then threatens to pull out unless the seller accepts a lower price. Happens in a falling market, is the opposite of **gazumping** and is legal at any time between offer and exchange.

Ground rent   A small annual payment, usually about £50 to £100, payable by **leaseholders** to their **freeholder**, for the 'rent' of their share of the land and property owned by the freeholder.

Homebuyer's report   A type of property survey less detailed than a full **structural survey** but more detailed than a **valuation survey**.

Index-tracker   A mortgage rate which moves up and down with base rates but which is set at a specified margin above base rates for a certain period.

Interest only mortgage   Monthly repayments are made up of interest only with premiums or contributions paid into a separate investment to pay off the capital.

Inventory   List of all landlord's possessions in a rented out property signed and agreed by landlord and tenant.

Joint sole agency   Two agents market the property jointly and split the commission.

Leasehold   Occupation of a property for a certain number of years as specified in a lease. Technically, leaseholders are tenants, not owner occupiers, with the owner legally being the **freeholder**. A lease is a legal document setting out the rights and obligations of landlord and tenant with regard to repairs, insurance and **ground rent**.

Leasehold valuation tribunal   Has powers to investigate disputes between **freeholders** and **leaseholders** including disputes over service charges. Also has the power to appoint a new manager if leaseholders can show the existing one is negligent, incompetent or dishonest.

Loan to value (LTV)   The proportion of the property's value borrowed as a mortgage. A 90 per cent LTV means 90 per cent of the property's price is being borrowed.

Local search   Information sought from local authorities by the buyer's solicitor during the housebuying process. Questions concern the property itself and proposals for the local area.

Lock-out agreement   Agreement signed by a seller and buyer in which the seller agrees to take his property off the market for a set period in return for an **exchange of contracts** during that period.

Mortgage indemnity guarantee (MIG)   Extra premium levied by mortgage brokers on borrowers needing a large proportion of the property's value, normally over 90 per cent. The premium pays for insurance to cover the lender if the property has to be repossessed and sold at a loss.

Mortgage in principle   Indication from a mortgage lender to a borrower that he or she is good for a loan judging by information supplied on income and credit history. A final mortgage **offer** depends on a satisfactory property valuation.

Mortgage payment protection insurance   Covers mortgage payments in the event of accident, sickness or unemployment.

Multiple agency   The property is marketed by several agents and whichever sells the property gets the commission.

Negative equity   A mortgage **secured** on the property is higher than the property's value. Happens when house prices fall sharply to buyers who have bought at the top of the market and borrowed a large proportion of the property's value.

Offer   The process of deciding to buy a property and naming your price. This can be the **asking price** or a lower or higher price. The offer marks the start of the **conveyancing** process.

Offplan   The process of buying a new property from floorplans and brochures because the actual property is not yet built.

Part-exchange A developer takes your current home and sells it on for you so that you can buy a new built home.

Permitted development rights Rights to carry out certain specified alterations or extensions without needing planning permission.

Redemption penalty Sum payable on certain mortgage deals for cashing in the loan before the end of a set period.

Repayment mortgage Loan repayments are a mixture of capital and interest and the mortgage is guaranteed to be paid off at the end of the term.

Restrictive covenant Clause in legal document, normally a lease or title deed, setting out what an owner or tenant cannot do in his property.

Sealed bids See **best and final offers**.

Secured loan Mortgage or other loan backed by property, allowing the lender to repossess the property to pay off the loan if payments aren't made.

Self-certification loan Mortgage granted without need for proof of income.

Seller's market When demand for property is high and buyers are willing to pay top prices. The opposite of a **buyer's market**.

Seller's pack A government proposal to speed up the housebuying process by requiring sellers to put together a pack of information on their properties before marketing them. Information will include **title deeds**, **leases**, **local searches** and a **homebuyer's report**.

Service charges Charges levied on tenants of leasehold properties for repairs, maintenance and insurance of the building. Normally payable annually but there may be extra demands for funds when major repairs are needed. Some leases provide for contributions to a **sinking fund**.

Sinking fund A fund built up by leaseholders through regular contributions to cover the cost of repairs and maintenance. The fund should be held in trust in a separate account by the landlord or his agent.

Sitting tenant   Tenant on 'fair' rent who cannot normally be evicted as long as as he or she pays rent and keeps to the tenancy agreement. Also known as statutory or protected tenant.

Sole agency   A single estate agent has the right to market the property, normally for a set period of time. The agent isn't liable for commission if the property is sold to someone not introduced by the agent.

Sole selling rights   An agent secures the right to sell a property and earn commission regardless of who actually sells it.

Stamp duty   A government tax levied on the purchase of all properties changing hands for more than £60,000. The tax is banded, with properties bought for between £60,001 and £250,000 charged at 1 per cent of the purchase price, properties between £250,001 and £500,000, 3 per cent and above £500,000, 4 per cent.

Standard variable rate (SVR)   The standard mortgage rate, usually a percentage point or so higher than the bank base rate. Moves up and down in line with base rates.

Structural survey   A detailed survey of the condition of a property including drains, cellars, lofts, roofs, wiring and brickwork. The most expensive type of survey available to homebuyers.

Title deeds   Legal documents which set out the ownership of a property. They include office copies of Land Registry entries for registered land (most land is registered), the deeds to unregistered land and other legal papers relating to the property like leases, guarantees and plans. If the property is mortgaged, the title deeds are held by the lender.

Valuation   The process of putting a price on a property. Used both by agents to set an **asking price** for marketing and selling and by surveyors doing valuation surveys to assess whether a property is worth the money a mortgage lender has been asked to lend.

Walk around tour   Recent technological innovation allowing online viewing of whole properties photographed with 360° degree camera.

USEFUL WEBSITES

Local government/local area sites

The Local Government Association **www.lganet.gov.uk**

Confederation of Scottish Local Authorities **www.cosla.gov.uk**

Department for Education and Skills **www.dfes.gov.uk**

Ofsted **www.ofsted.gov.uk**

Greater London Authority **www.london.gov.uk**

The Environment Agency **www.environment-agency.gov.uk**

www.upmystreet.com

www.yell.com

www.homecheckuk.com

www.ukonline.gov.uk

www.streetmap.co.uk

House prices

Halifax **www.halifax.co.uk**

Nationwide **www.nationwide.co.uk**

Land Registry **www.landreg.gov.uk**

Property search sites

www.reapit.com for reviews of property websites

See also Chapter 2 sites

Buying agents

Knight Frank **www.knightfrank.com**
FPD Savills **www.fpdsavills.co.uk**
Home Search Bureau **www.homesearchbureau.com**

Chapter 2: Selling

The property industry/government departments

The National Association of Estate Agents **www.naea.org.uk**
The Royal Institution of Chartered Surveyors **www.rics.org.uk**
The Estate Agents Ombudsman Scheme **www.oea.co.uk**
The Office of Fair Trading **www.oft.gov.uk**
The Department of Transport, Local Government and the Regions
www.dtlr.gov.uk

Property search sites

www.hometrack.co.uk
www.rightmove.co.uk
www.assertahome.co.uk
www.fish4.co.uk
www.propertyfinder.co.uk
www.primelocation.com
www.findaproperty.com
www.o8oo4homes.co.uk
www.thisislondon.co.uk

House doctor

www.thefinaltouch.co.uk

209

Chapter 3: The buying and selling process

England and Wales

The Law Society **www.lawsoc.org.uk**

The Council of Mortgage Lenders **www.cml.org.uk**

Inland Revenue **www.inlandrevenue.co.uk**

www.freelawyer.co.uk

Scotland

Law Society of Scotland **www.scotlaw.org.uk**

Leasehold/freehold

Lease **www.lease-advice.org**

Coalition for the Abolition of Residential Leasehold (CARL)
www.carl.org.uk

Department of Transport, Local Government and the Regions
www.dtlr.gov.uk

Association of Residential Managing Agents **www.arma.org.uk**

Online conveyancing

National Land Information Service **www.nlis.org.uk**

Lord Chancellor's Department **www.territorium.co.uk**

Moving costs

Woolwich **www.woolwich.co.uk**

Chapter 4: Your finances

Government departments/regulators/advice

Department of Trade and Industry **www.dti.gov.uk**

Treasury **www.hmtreasury.gov.uk**

Financial Services Authority **www.fsa.gov.uk**

National Association of Citizens' Advice Bureaux **www.nacab.org.uk**

Mortgage Code Compliance Board **www.mortgagecode.org.uk**

Consumers Association **www.which.net**

National Consumer Council **www.ncc.org.uk**

Financial Ombudsman Service **www.financial-ombudsman.org.uk**

Chartered Institute of Arbitrators **www.arbitrators.org**

Association of British Insurers **www.abi.org.uk**

Online mortgage search sites/brokers

Moneyfacts **www.moneyfacts.co.uk**

www.find.co.uk

www.moneysupermarket.co.uk

www.moneynet.co.uk

www.moneyextra.com

John Charcol of **www.charcol-online.co.uk**

London and Country Mortgages **www.lcplc.co.uk**

Chapter 5: New homes

New homes warranties/consumer groups

NHBC **www.nhbc.co.uk**

Zurich Municipal **www.zurich.co.uk**

National Association of New Homeowners **www.nanho.org.uk**

New homes property search

www.freeagents.co.uk

www.newhomesnetwork.co.uk

See also sites listed in Chapters 1 and 2

Self build

www.homebuilding.co.uk

www.plotfinder.net

www.buildstore.co.uk

www.ebuild.co.uk

Chapter 6: Moving house and home improvements

Removals and storage listings/businesses

The British Association of Removers **www.bar.co.uk**

Thomsons Directories **www.thomweb.co.uk**

Big Yellow Self-Storage **www.thebigyellow.co.uk**

Removals/change of address sites

www.reallymoving.com

www.ihavemoved.com

www.simplymove.co.uk

www.royalmail.com

Planning/ home improvements/restoration

The Royal Town Planning Institute **www.rtpi.org.uk**

The Royal Institute of British Architects **www.architecture.com**

Society for the Protection of Ancient Buildings **www.spab.org.uk**

English Heritage **www.english-heritage.org.uk**

SAVE Britain's Heritage **www.savebritainsheritage.org**

Chapter 7: Renting and letting

Association of Residential Letting Agents (ARLA) **www.arla.co.uk**

www.buytolet.co.uk

Specialist rental property sites

www.easylet.org

www.letonthenet.com

www.lettingweb.com

Chapter 8: Off the wall

House swapping

www.webswappers.com

Auctions

www.propwatch.com

Overseas property agents

Hamptons International **www.hamptons.co.uk**

Knight Frank **www.knightfrank.com**

FPD Savills **www.fpdsavills.co.uk**

Property search sites

www .french-property-news.com

www.french-property.com

www.europropertynet.com

www.spanishpropertyco.com

www.cornishco.com

INDEX

Abbey National 103
accident, sickness and unemployment (ASU)
    insurance 116
aggregated sites, 44–5, definition 201
Alliance & Leicester, buy to let 180
Alternative Investment Market 43
appliances 174, 176–7
area gentrification 9–12
    signs 10–12
area research 3–9
    top tips 4–5
    Web Watch 5–9
ARLA *see* Association of Residential Letting
    Agents
arrangement fees 91
    definition 201
Association of British Insurers 116
Association of New Homeowners 130
Association of Residential Letting Agents
    (ARLA) 165, 175
    buying to let 181–2
    deposits 165, 171
assured shorthold tenancy 169
    definition 201
assured tenancy 169–70
    definition 201
ASU *see* accident, sickness and unemployment
    insurance
auctions 191–6
    buying 191–3
    selling 193–5
    Web Watch 195–6

banks and building societies 103–4
BAR *see* British Association of Removers
Barclays 103
Barnes, Yolande 10, 12
Barratt Homes 128
bathroom 46, 146–9
best and final offer 27–8
    definition 201
Big Yellow Self-Storage 142
Birmingham 120
boilers and heating equipment 167–8
boom market 27–8
bridging loan 139–40
    definition 201
Bristol 10, 120

British Association of Removers (BAR)
    142–3
Brown, Gordon 74
brownfield sites 120–1
Buildmark policy 131
buy to let 180–4
    ARLA dos and don'ts 181–2
    definition 201
    investment priorities 182–3
    property choice 180–2
    property investment calculator 183
    tax matters 184
    Web Watch 182
Buy To Let scheme 180
buyer 13
    survey 67–8
    valuation 56–8, 67, 69–70
buying xv, 1–28
    area gentrification 9–12
    area research 3–9
    estate agents 12–19
    househunting 3
    mortgage 2
    offer making 27–8
    price indices 20–1
    property viewing 21–6
    useful websites 208–9
buying agent
    FPD Savills 26
    Home Search Bureau 26
    Knight Frank 26
buying and selling (England and Wales)
    56–74
    buyer 67–9
    exchange and completion 72–4
    leasehold vs freehold 62–6
    offer 56
    solicitors 58–62
    Stamp Duty 74
    survey results 70–1
    valuations action point 56–8
    Web Watch 62
buying and selling process 54–81
    costs 57–8
    England and Wales 56–74
    future system (England and Wales) 75–7
    Scotland 78–81
    useful websites 210

buying and selling (Scotland) 78–81
  acceptance 80
  bargain 80
  burdens and servitudes 80
  conveyancing 80
  date of entry 80
  disposition 80–1
  finance 79
  househunting 79
  missive 80
  mortgage 79–80
  offer 80
  property enquiry certificate 80
  signature 81

capital gains tax 184
capped rate mortgage 87–8
  definition 202
Cardiff 10, 120
CARL see Coalition for the Abolition of
    Residential Leasehold
CAT marks 94–5
  definition 202
  fixed/capped rate 94
  mortgage cost 95
  variable rate 94
chain xii
  definition 202
Chartered Institute of Arbitrators 111
checklist 91–4
  arrangement fees 91
  compulsory insurance 93–4
  mortgage indemnity guarantee (MIG) 93
  penalties for early redemption 92–3
  valuation fees 91–2
closed loan 139–40
Clydesdale Bank, buy to let 180
CML see Council of Mortgage Lenders
Coalition for the Abolition of Residential
    Leasehold (CARL) 66
commission 41–2
Commonhold and Leasehold Reform bill 64
complaints procedure 111
completion 73–4, 139–40
  date 59
complex case 95–8
compulsory insurance 93–4
condensation/damp 168
conservation areas 150–1
conservatory 146–9
Consumer Protection (Distance Selling)
    Regulations xviii
contract 72–3
CORGI-registered engineer 168, 176
Council of Mortgage Lenders (CML) 70, 92–3,
    97–8, 109–10, 116

Countrywide Property Auctions 191, 193
creditworthiness 2, 113–14

Daily Telegraph 52
Department of Trade and Industry (DTI),
    checklist 91
Department of Transport, Local Government
    and the Regions xiii, 164, 170
deposits 165, 170–1
  definition 203
  lettings agents 165
discount mortgage 88
  definition 203
discrimination 163–4
DIY moves 141–2
  cons 141–2
  pros 141
do-it-yourself-shared-ownership (DIYSO) 97
double glazing 47, 147–9
draft contract 59
  definition 203
DTI see Department of Trade and Industry

e-conveyancing 77
Electronic Communications Act 2000 77
endowment 100–2
  definition 203
England and Wales xi
  future system 75–7
  see also buying and selling
English Heritage 153
estate agent 12–19
  charges 41–2
  choice 32–3
  commission 41–2
  getting the best 13–14
  marketing 33
  mortgage suppliers 104
  Top Tips 32–3
  Web Watch 15–19
  websites 33, 43–4
Estate Agents Act 1979 51
Estate Agents Ombudsman Scheme 32–3
Evening Standard 52

Fairview New Homes 128
fees and deposits 170–1
  deposits 170–1
  fees 170
finances 82–116
  CAT marks 94–5
  checklist 91–4
  complex case 95–8
  investment type 99–102
  loan application 112–15
  Mortgage Code 112

finances *continued*
　mortgage market 84–5
　mortgage products 85–91
　mortgage regulation 109–11
　mortgage repayment protection 115–16
　mortgage suppliers 103–8
　remortgaging 114–15
　repayment methods 98–9
　useful websites 211
Financial Ombudsman Service 111
Financial Services Authority (FSA) xviii,
　109–10
　complaints 111
fire regulations 174
fixed rate mortgage 87
　definition 203
flexible mortgage 89
　definition 203
FPD Savills 10, 26
freehold xi
　definition 203
　see also leasehold
FSA *see* Financial Services Authority
FTB (first time buyer) 15
Fulham 10
Furniture and Fittings (Fire) (Safety)
　Regulations 1988 176

garage 148
garden 46, 147–9
gazumping
　definition 204
　xiii, auctions 192
gazundering xiii
　definition 204
going it alone 52–3
Greater London Authority (GLA) 42
greenfield sites 121

Halifax 20, 103, 147–8
Halifax Mortgage Services, buy to let 180
Hamptons International, fees 170
HB *see* housing benefit
home improvements 146–9
　top 147–9
Home Search Bureau 26
home security 147–9
Homebuy scheme 97
homebuyer/flatbuyer report 68–70
　definition 204
Homes Bill 48
HOT (hot prospects) 15
house swapping 188–91
　moneysaving 189–90
　Web Watch 190–1
househunting 3

Housing Act 1988 157, 178, 180
Housing Act 1996 64, 169
housing benefit (HB) 164

IFAs *see* independent financial advisers
inclusive/exclusive rents 161
Independent 52
independent financial advisers (IFAs) 105
index-tracker 88
　definition 204
individual savings account (ISA) 100–1
Inland Revenue
　buy to let 184
　house swapping 190
internet, impact xvi
internet letting 166–7
　Web Watch 166–7
internet loan 113
internet mortgage 105–8
internet selling 42–5
　aggregated sites 44–5
　estate agent websites 43–4
inventories 171–2
　definition 204
investment priorities 182–3
investment type 99–102
　endowment 100
　individual savings account (ISA) 100–1
　pension 101
ISA *see* individual savings account
Islington 10

joint sole agency 41
　definition 204

kitchen 46, 146–9
Knight Frank 26

Land Registry xii, 20–1, 48, 59, 75–6
landlords 173–90
　agent 174–5
　own home let 174
　preparing property 173–4
　property vacation 177–8
　repossession 178–80
　safety regulations 176–7
landlords vs tenants 159
Law Society 57
leasehold xi
　accounts/service charges 65
　common parts 65
　definition 204
　landlord's record 65
　lease length 65
　solicitor 65
leasehold valuation tribunal (LVT) 64

leasehold vs freehold 62–6
  Web Watch 66
Leeds 10, 120, 148
letting *see* renting and letting
lettings agents 164–5, 168, 174–5
  cons 175
  deposits 165
  pros 175
lifestyle selling 128–30
listed buildings 152–3
Listed Buildings Information Service 152
Liverpool 120
Lloyds TSB 103
loan application 112–15
  creditworthiness 113–14
  internet 113
  in person 112–13
  remortgaging 114–15
  telephone 113
location 34
lock-out agreement 27
  definition 205
loft conversion 47, 146–9
Loot 52
Lorentzen, Chris 130

Manchester 10, 120, 148
market type 39–40
  balanced market 39
  buyer's market 39
  seller's market 39
MIG *see* mortgage indemnity guarantee
mortgage xv, 2
  creditworthiness 2
  self-employed 2
  solicitor 59
Mortgage Code 112
Mortgage Code Compliance Board 110–11
mortgage cost 95
Mortgage Express, buy to let 180
mortgage indemnity guarantee (MIG) 93
  definition 205
mortgage market 84–5
mortgage products 85–91
  capped rate 87–8
  discount 88
  fixed rate 87
  flexible 89
  index-tracker 88
  search 90
  variable or standard variable rate (SVR) 86–7
  Web Watch 91
mortgage regulation 109–11
  complaints procedure 111
mortgage repayment protection 115–16
mortgage suppliers 103–8

banks and building societies 103–4
  estate agents 104
  independent financial advisers (IFAs) 105
  internet 105–8
moving arrangements 138–40
moving house and home improvements 136–53
  completion 139–40
  home improvements 146–9
  moving arrangements 138–40
  moving tasks 140
  planning matters 149–50
  planning permission 150–3
  removals 141–4
  useful websites 212–13
  utilities 144–6
moving tasks 140
multiple agency 41
  definition 205

National Association of Citizens' Advice
  Bureaux (NACAB) 97
  deposit disputes 171
National Association of Estate Agents (NAEA)
  27, 32
National House Building Council (NHBC)
  130–1
  warranty 130–1
National Land Information Service (NLIS) 75
Nationwide 20
NatWest Mortgage Services, buy to let 180
new build buying system 122–4
  part-exchange 128
  Web Watch 126–7
new homes xv, 118–35
  buying 120–1
  lifestyle selling 128–30
  new build buying system 122–4
  self-build 132–3
  showhouse trade tricks 125–6
  state of play 120–1
  useful websites 211–12
  warranty 130–2
newspapers and magazines 52
NHBC *see* National House Building Council
NLIS *see* National Land Information Service
NTS (nothing to sell) 15

off the wall 186–200
  auctions 191–6
  house swapping 188–91
  overseas buying 196–200
  useful websites 213–14
offer 49–53
  asking price 50–1
  definition 205
  less than asking price 49

offer making 27–8
   best and final offer 27–8
   boom market 27–8
   lock-out agreement 27
   sealed bid 27–8
   static market 27
Office of Fair Trading (OFT) xvii, 51
offplan buying 122
   definition 205
100 per cent loan 96
online security xvii
overseas buying 196–200
   tips 197–8
   Web Watch 198–200

Paragon Mortgages, buy to let 180
part-exchange 128
   definition 206
penalties for early redemption 92–3
pension 101
periodic tenancy 169
planning matters 149–50
planning permission 150–3
   conservation areas 150–1
   listed buildings 152–3
   permitted development rights 151
playing by the rules 1–2
price 37–8
price indices 20–1
   Halifax 20
   Land Registry 20–1
   Nationwide 20
professional removers 142–4
   cons 143
   pros 142
   Web Watch 143–4
property advertising
   internet 166–7
   letting 162–7
   lettings agents 164–5
   newspapers & magazines 162–3
property choice, buy to let 180–2
property investment calculator 183
Property Misdescriptions Act 1993 51
property search, tenants 159–61
property value 34–8
   price 37–8
   valuation 35–7
   Web Watch 36
property viewing 21–6
   buying agent 26
   letting 167–8
   tenants 167–8
   think location 22–3
   think owner 24–6
   think property 23–4

questionnaire (seller) 59–61

Rachman, Peter 157, 174
redecorating 46
references 168
remortgaging 114–15
removals 141–4
   DIY moves 141–2
   professional removers 142–4
Rent Act 1977 177
rent assessment committee 177
renting xv, 156–8
   history 157–8
   Housing Act 1988 157
renting and letting 154–84
   buy to let 180–4
   history 157–8
   landlords 173–90
   landlords vs tenants 159
   renting xv, 156–8
   tenants 159–73
   useful websites 213
rents 161–2
   inclusive/exclusive 161
   weekly/monthly 161
repayment methods 98–9
   interest-only loan 99
   repayment loan 98–9
repossession 178–80
   assured shorthold tenancies 178
   assured tenancies 178
   sitting tenants 177–8
research see area research
Royal Institute of British Architects (RIBA),
   Clients Advisory Service 150
Royal Institution of Chartered Surveyors (RICS)
   32, 69
   new homes 132
Royal Mail 146

safety regulations 176–7
saleability creation 45–9
   bathroom 46
   double glazing 47
   garden 46
   kitchen 46
   loft conversion 47
   redecorating 46
SAVE Britain's Heritage 153
Scotland xi
   offer making 28
   see also buying and selling
sealed bid 27–8
   definition 206
searches xii, 61
self-build 132–3

self-build *continued*
  Web Watch 133–5
self-certification loan 96
  definition 206
sellers' packs 48–9, 60–1, 69–70
  definition 206
selling xv, 30–53
  estate agent charges 41–2
  estate agent choice 32–3
  going it alone 52–3
  internet selling 42–5
  market type 39–40
  offer 49–53
  playing by the rules 51–2
  property value 34–8
  saleability creation 45–9
  sellers' packs 48–9
  terms 40–1
  useful websites 209
share of freehold (SoF) 66
shared ownership 96–7
showhouse trade tricks 125–6
sitting tenants 177–8
  definition 207
Social and Community Planning Research
  164
Society for the Protection of Ancient Buildings
  (SPAB) 153
sole agency 40
  definition 207
sole selling rights 40–1
  definition 207
solicitors xi–xii, 58–62
  choice 57
  fees 57
  legal stages 58–62
  overseas buying 198
  seller's pack 60–1
  Web Watch 62
stamp duty 38, 74
  definition 207
  house swapping 190
standard variable rate (SVR) 86–7
  definition 207
static market 27
stress xi–xii
structural survey 68
  definition 207
Sunday Telegraph 52
Sunday Times 152
survey 67–8
  homebuyer/flatbuyer report 68
  structural 68
SVR *see* standard rate variable
sweep facility 89

tax matters, buy to let 184
tenancy
  obligations 173
  rights 173
tenancy agreement 169–70
  assured 169–70
  assured shorthold 169
tenants 159–73
  fees and deposits 170–1
  inventories 171–2
  property advertising 162–7
  property search 159–61
  property viewing 167–8
  references 168
  rents 161–2
  tenancy agreement 169–70
  tenancy rights 173
Teramedia 77
terms 40–1
  joint sole agency 41
  multiple agency 41
  sole agency 40
  sole selling rights 40–1
think location 22–3
think owner 24–6
think property 23–4
Times 52
timescale xiii
title deeds xii, 58–9
  definition 207
TrustUK xviii

utilities 144–6
  Royal Mail 146
  Web Watch 145–6

valuation 35–7, 56–8, 67, 69–70
  definition 207
  fees 91–2
value *see* property value
variable or standard variable rate (SVR)
  86–7
viewing *see* property viewing

warranty 130–2
websites
  council 5–6
  government 6
  Greater London Authority 11
  see also Web Watch
weekly/monthly rents 161
Which magazine 110
Woolwich Bank 56–7

Zurich Municipal 131